PREFACE.

I0153441

Custom, if not utility, has rendered necessary a preface ever since books were first printed. It is to a publisher what a prologue is to a play; the one serves to please an auditor, the other suits for an apology or an explanation to the reader. In the present case, apology is not sought after; but an opportunity is merely taken in a part of this preface, to account for any and perhaps several errors which may appear in the following pages.

To the intelligent, little need be said of the many great difficulties attending the making of a Directory; however, to mention a few, and how they have been overcome, may not be improper. Many, at first, through a misconception of the intention of the publisher, refused to give their names altogether; and, in some cases, the names and vocations of the inhabitants have been received through children or servants; and, as there are no established rules for spelling proper names, many have probably been misspelt.

Some may, perhaps, object to the price of this little work, on account of its size, but it is hoped that the smallness of the type, the condensation of the matter by abbreviations, and the quality rather than the quantity of matter will be considered in the estimation of its value: for many volumes, of double its size will be found less useful: besides, it should be remembered, that *every line* has cost a short walk, and was attended with some trouble.

Explanation of the Abbreviations, &c.

F street north, is expressed by Fn; south, by Fs; Seventh street west, by 7w; east, by 7e: the word *street* being always understood.

All the other streets are designated in the same method; dw. is for dwelling;—btw between. The other contractions, it is thought, need no explanation.—It is hoped that the Corporation will cause to be erected street sign-boards, at the corners of nearly all the squares, and at the junctions of streets, &c.

It may afford satisfaction to those unacquainted with the plan of the City of Washington, to state, that all the streets running east and west are named by the letters of the English alphabet; and that they are called north or south streets, according as they are situated north or south of the Capitol, which is the dividing point; as, A street north, and A street south, which are the nearest streets north and south of the Capitol.

Those streets running north and south, are named numerically, and are designated by the word east or west, as they are situated east or west of the Capitol; as, First street east, and First street west, &c.

The grand avenues, and such streets as lead immediately to public places, are from 120 to 160 feet wide. The other streets are from 90 to 112 feet wide. North and South Capitol streets, each 130 feet wide; East Capitol street, 160; "Half streets," east and west, 80; Four-and-a-half street west, 110; Thirteen-and-a-half street west, 70; Water street, 60; and Canal street, 80 feet wide.

In order to execute this plan, Mr. ELLICOTT drew a true meridional line, by celestial observa-

THE WASHINGTON DIRECTORY

SHOWING THE

NAME, OCCUPATION, AND RESIDENCE

OF EACH

𝕳𝖊𝖆𝖉 𝖔𝖋 𝖆 𝕱𝖆𝖒𝖎𝖑𝖞 &
𝕻𝖊𝖗𝖘𝖔𝖓 𝖎𝖓 𝕭𝖚𝖘𝖎𝖓𝖊𝖘𝖘

TOGETHER WITH
OTHER USEFUL INFORMATION

—CITY OF WASHINGTON—

Originally Printed
and Published by
S. A. Elliot
1827

HERITAGE BOOKS
2012

tion, which passed through the centre area intended for the centre of the Capitol. This line he crossed by another, due east and west, which passed through the same point.

The credit of laying out this city on its extensive scale, belongs certainly to General WASHINGTON and Major L'ENFANT. And the building of the Capitol, where it now stands, completely elevated above all other edifices within the boundaries, was at the instance of the General.

The city is divided into the following wards:

First Ward.—All that part of the city to the westward of Fifteenth street west.

Second Ward.—That part of the city between Fifteenth and Tenth streets west.

Third Ward.—That part between Tenth and First streets west, and north of E street south.

Fourth Ward.—That part between First street west and Eighth street east, and north of E street south.

Fifth Ward.—That part between Tenth street west and Fourth street east, and south of E street south.

Sixth Ward.—The residue of the city.

It appears by the census taken in this city in 1820, that it contained 13,474 persons; and it contains, in the present year, (1827) it is supposed, in round numbers, about 16,500; making an increase of population in seven years of 3,026 persons.

As a closing paragraph to these remarks, the publisher hopes that for any errors or omissions, the propriety of attempting to do justice to the undertaking, will apologize for any want of correctness in its execution. S. A. E.

CHANGES AND OMISSIONS.

ANDERSON, WILLIAM, clk 1st comptroller's office, dw w side 7w btw E and Fn

Archer, William, carpenter, w side 12w btw E and Fn

Ashbaugh, John, paver, w side 7w near Hn

Baker, John H. clk in clerk's office of the circuit court; dw North Capitol st btw B and Cn

Baker, Rev. Daniel, Ln btw 14 and 15w

Barrell, Samuel B. attorney at law, house and office removed to 15w near Bank United States.

Belt, Levin, clk 4th auditor's office; dw I n near west mark't

Bolden, Alexander, carpenter, near corner Ln and 15w

Bradley, Joseph S. attorney at law, n side Dn btw 6 and 7w

Brashears, Noah, teacher, I n btw 17 and 18w

Broom, Charles R. captain marines, Gs near marine barracks

Burr, Richard R. jailor, En north of city hall

Cathcart, James L. clk in 2d comptroller's office; dw 17w btw I and Kn

Chapman, Sidney F. clk 2d comptroller's office; dw at Mrs. King's, e side 14w btw Pen av and Fn

Cutts, James M. clk 2d comptroller's office; dw Hn near St. John's church

Easton, William C. clk com. gen. of subsistence; dw at Mrs. Smoot's, near war office

Graham, Mrs. J. G. widow, removed to s w corner 14w and M n

Hook, Major J. H. clk com. gen. of subsistence; dw Fn btw 13 and 14w

Hunt, Captain Thomas, clk com. gen. of subsistence; dw n side Fn btw 19 and 20w

Laurie, William S. merchant, Dn near Pen av and corner of ner 12w

Lowe, John H. clk 2d comptroller's office; dw at J. A. Wilson's, corner of 14w and Gn

Mason, Richard B corner 14w and Hn

Mitchell, John, clk com gen. of subsistence

Nally, Aaron, carpenter, 8w btw D and En

Phillips, William, printer, e side 10w btw D and En

Reed, Josiah, printer, e side 11w btw Pen av and En

Reitz, Frederick, glass-blower, n side Pen av btw 15 & 14w

Reynolds, Enoch, ch clk 2d comptroller's office; dw N York av btw 13 and 14w

Rhodes, Sam'l hardware & cutlery store, corner Pen av & 9w

Seaver, Jonathan, clk 2d compt's office; dw 7w btw D & En

Smith, William S clk   do.   dw at Mrs. Freeman's, 7 buildings, Pen avenue

Tree, Lambert, mess. "*city*" post office: dw Fn near 7w

WASHINGTON DIRECTORY.

☞ *For explanation of abbreviations, see* **Preface.**

RESIDENTS.

ABBOT, John, clk in third auditor's office; dw **Georgetown**

Abbot, Joseph, hackman, n w corner Fn and 13w

Achman, Mrs. widow, Hn btw 19 and 20w

Acken, William, shipwright, corner 9e and Ms N Yard

Adams, John Quincy, President of the United States, at the President's mansion

Adams, Mrs. widow, 14e near Eastern Branch

Adams, Rebecca, widow, Bn btw 3 and 4e Capitol Hill

Adams, Margaret, widow, Ds btw 3 and 4e

Adams, Joseph, carpenter, 13½w btw C and Ds

Adams, Thomas, chairmaker, s side Pen av btw 12 and 13w

Adams, George, collector 5th and 6th wards, 8e btw K & Ls

Adams, George, police officer, corner 4e and Ls

Adams, John, bricklayer, Gn btw 17 and 18w

Addison, Thomas B. clk in general post office; dw Georgetown

Addison, W. D. clk in general post office; dw Pr. George's county, Md.

Agg, John, writer, Mrs. M'Cauley's, Pen av

Aiken, Prudence, widow, n side Cn btw 4½ and 6w

Alexander, Charles, upholsterer, n side Pen av btw 12 & 13w

2

Alexander, Miss Nelly, Ns btw 4½ and Union st Greenleaf's Point

Allen, Rev, Ethan, pastor of Christ's Church, Gs btw 6 and 7e N. Yard; dw rear of the church

Allen, Robert, carpenter, n w corner En and 13w

Allen, John, dry goods' store, n side Pen av btw 11 and 12w

Allen, S. & M. & Co. lottery and exchange brokers, n side Pen av a few doors west of the Indian Queen hotel

Allen, James, grocer, w side 8e near E Branch

Allen, Nasi, 1s btw 3 and 4e

Allen, Ann, widow, s w corner 4e and As

Allison, William S. clk pension office; dw Gay st Georgetown

Anderson, Joseph, first comptroller; dw w side 7w btw E and Fn

Anderson, William, clk 1st comptroller's office; dw 6w btw E and Fn

Anderson, Thomas F. clk 1st comptroller's office; dw at Mrs. Ball's, s side Pen. av. btw 6 and 7w

Anderson, William, blacksmith, Gn btw 21 and 22w

Anderson, James, shoemaker, En btw 9 and 19w

Andrews, Christopher, clk 3d auditor's office; dw n w corner Gn and 10w

Andrews, Timothy P. Brown's hotel

Andre, S. D. consul of France, n e corner Pen av and 14w

Anthony, James L. clk office of the secretary of the treasury; dw at Tilley's Union Tavern, Georgetown

Appler, David, proprietor of the Fountain Inn, n e corner Pen av and 12w

Arbuckle, Thomas, clk gen post office; dw Gn btw 17 & 18w

Archer, James, carpenter, w side 12w btw E and Fn

Ardry, Mrs. (col woman) widow, near the glass house

Arden, Daniel D. agent for Yates and M'Intyre, lottery brokers, Pen av opposite Brown's hotel

Arguelles, Elizabeth Theresa, widow, boarding house, s w corner Pen av and 9w

Armistead, Robert, carpenter, Geo av near N Yard

Armstead, Robert, master caulker at navy yard; dw 9e btw L and Ms N Yard

Armstrong, Walter, founder, s w corner Is and 11e N Yard

Armstrong, Andrew, hairdresser, Ls btw 7 and 8e N Yard

Arny, Joseph, confectioner, Pen av. next to corner 9w

Ashburn, John, paver, w side 7w near Hn

Ashman, Mary, widow, Md av btw 3 and 4½w

Ashton, Henry, attorney at law, s e corner En and 13w

Ashton, C. H. B. timber merchant, 8e opp marine barracks, N Yard

Awkward, Ann, washerwoman, 6e near E. Branch, N Yard

Awkward, H. shoemaker, n side Ls btw 7 and 8e N Yard

Attkinson, John, lamplighter, Bn btw 6 and 7w

Ault, Henry, tinman, n side Pen av btw 8 and 9w

B.

BACKER, THOMAS, hack driver, 26w btw I and Kn

Bacon, Samuel, grocer, s e corner Pen av and 7w opposite centre market

Bage, William, modeller, and ornamental plasterer, N Yk av west of the navy department

Bailey, John, messenger 3d auditor's office; dw w side 7w next corner Gn

Bailey, John, saddler, n e corner Gn and 13w

Bailey, William, laborer, 11e near Bs N Yard

Baker, Rev. Daniel, pastor second Presbyterian church; dw w side 12w btw G and Hn

Baker, John M. clk secretary of state's office; dw 13w btw E & Fn

Ball, Henry W. clk in 5th auditor's office; dw corner Bn and 1e Cap Hill

Ball, Mrs. Miriam, boarding-house, Pen av btw 6 and 7w

Ballard, Charles, dw ne corner 8w and Dn.

Baldwin, Ethan, overseer Washington canal, So Cap st near 1st Presbyterian church

Baldwin, Margaret, widow, Is btw 3 and 4e

Banckhead, Charles, 1st door east of 6 buildings, Pen av

Barbour, James, secretary of war; dw En btw 6 and 7w

Barclay, Thomas, clk first auditor's office; dw corner 20w and Mn

Barclay, John D. clk register's office; dw 18w near Pen av

Barcroft, John, n e corner 20w and In

Barcroft, Titus, carpenter, 7e btw K and Ls N Yard

Barnhill, Gabriel, printer, e side 8w btw G and Hn

Barrell, Samuel B. attorney at law; dw Kn btw 25 and 26w; office opposite treasury department

Barron, James, messenger clk's office, H. of Representatives dw south, fronting capitol square

Barron, Henry, carpenter, Gn btw 11 and 12w

Barron, James, bricklayer, 11w btw G and Hn

Barron, Mary, widow, e side 11w btw G and Hn

Barry, capt. Edward, sailing master at N Yard; dw in Yard

Barry, Edward, turner, n side Pen av btw 4½ and 6w; dw at Mrs. Arguelles'

Barry, Elizabeth, tavern, Louisiana av btw 6 and 7w

Barry, jr. Robert, clk 5th auditor's office, dw Georgetown

Barry, James, 3e near Eastern Branch

Barry, Francis, s e corner Ks and 10e N Yard

Barlow, John, (col. man) laborer, 12w near Tiber Creek

Barns, Jesse, mast maker at N Yard, 4e near E. Branch

Barns, William H. lumber measurer, 3e btw M and Ns

Barnes, William, attendant in the stage office, next door east of Brown's hotel

Barnes, Mary, sempstress, In btw 20 and 21w

Barrett, Catharine, widow, Pen av btw 1 and 2e Cap Hill

Bassett, Simeon, stone cutter, n side East Cap st near market, Cap Hill

Bates, Thomas, soap and candle manufactory, 7w btw F and Gn

Bates, Miss Julia, Vir av btw 7 and 8e N Yard

Bates, Ann, widow, 7e btw L and Ms

Baum, Catharine, widow, s e corner 6w and En
Bayley, Mountjoy, sergeant-at-arms of the Senate, n e cor-
  ner East Cap st and 2e Cap Hill
Bayne, John, carpenter, 3e btw M and Ns
Bayne, Thomas, shoemaker, 8e next to corner Ks N Yard
Bayne, H. T. merchant tailor, and boarding house keeper,
  Pen av btw 2 and 3w
Beall, Dr. J. H. east side N Jer av btw L and Ms N Yard
Beall, jr. George, purser in the navy, Fn btw 19 and 20w
Beall, Benjamin L. clk pension office; dw 19w btw F & Gn
Beall, Benjamin B. clk treasurer's office; dw 19w
Beall, Gideon, clk treasurer's office; dw N York av near 18w
Beall, Walter B. clk gen land office; dw at Mrs Pittman's, Fn
Beall, Thomas W. w side N. Jer av btw L and Ms
Beale, Robert, attorney at law, Louisiana av btw 6 and 7w
Bean, George, spar maker, 3e near the Eastern Branch
Bean, Benjamin, carpenter, corner.3e and Ls   do
Beardsley, Joseph, s e corner 18w and In
Beach, William, laborer, Geo av btw 11 and 12e N Yard
Beck, Lambert S. constable, 7w btw F and Gn
Beck, Joseph W. police officer, corner As and 3e Cap Hill
Bede, George, hackman, Pen av btw 17 and 18w
Beers, Isaac, tavern, 7w opposite centre market
Bell, Levin, clk 4th auditor's office; dw In near west mark't
Bell, John B. bookbinder, e side 9w btw D and En
Bell, John, carpenter, 8w btw G and Hn
Bell, Edward, East Cap st btw 1 and 2e Cap Hill
Bell, Charles, watchman gen post office; dw btw 9 and 10w
Bell, Cassey, widow, corner Mn and 18w
Bell, Alfred, lock maker, at N Yard, n side Vir av btw 6
  and 7e N Yard
Belt, Benjamin M. cabinet maker, n side Pen av btw 9 & 10w
Belt, Rebecca, widow, opposite marine barracks, N Yard
Bender, Jacob A. bricklayer, 9w btw E and Fn
  2*

Bender, George, 21w btw H and In

Benning, Mr. s side En btw 6 and 7w

Bentliff, Joseph, carpenter, 11w btw Pen av and En

Benting, Martha Ann, In btw 15 and 16w

Bernard, General, s w corner 18w and Gn; office 18w btw
    Pen av and Gn

Bernard, Henry, clk adjt general's office

Berry, Brook M. clk in office of clk House of Representa-
    tives; dw n side East Cap st opposite the market

Berry, George T. carpenter, s e corner 3e and East Cap
    st Cap Hill

Berry, Mary, boarding house, Lou av btw 6 and 7w

Berkley, Peter, 11e near bridge, N Yard

Bestor, Chauncey, clk gen post office; dw e side 11w btw
    G and Hn

Bestor, Harvey, boarding house, 1e rear of old capitol,
    Cap Hill

Betzold, Frederick, butcher, Union st Greenleaf's Point

Bezat, Charles, gardener, corner 6w and Vir av

Billings, W. W. collector 1st and 2d wards, e side 14w btw
    F and Gn

Birth, James, stone cutter, 8w btw D and En

Blackford, Frs. G. clk gen post office; dw Mrs. M'Cauley's

Black, Samuel, grocer, 7w opposite centre market

Blagrove, H. B. clk qr master general's office; dw Gn near
    Davidson's wharf

Blair, William, clk gen post office; dw 8w op post office

Blake, Mrs Dr. Jas. H. widow, n w corner 8w and Lou av.

Blake, John B., M. D.   ditto

Blanchard, Ann, widow, 8w opposite gen post office

Bland, Delila, widow, 10e opposite N Yard

Bockman, William, bricklayer, 28w near the Georgetown
    lower bridge

Bohleyr, John, butcher, s e corner 8e and Is N Yard

Bolden, Alexander, carpenter, near corner Mn and 14w

Bollinger, Conrad, gardener, e side 7w btw B and Cs

Bomford, Col. George, ordnance dept; dw Kalorama

Bonfils, S. F. s w corner Fn and 12w

Bond, Samuel, gardener, s e corner $4\frac{1}{2}$w and Md av

Boone, John F. clk gen post office; dw 7w btw I and Kn

Boone, Alexius, laborer, Ks btw 8 and 9e N Yard

Booth, Mordecai, clk to commandant of the N Yard; dw
Vir av btw 3 and 4e

Booth, Edward, sawyer at N Yard; dw 3e btw M and Ns

Booth, Mrs. widow, 3e btw M and Ns

Borrows, Joseph, messenger gen post office; dw n side En
btw 9 and 10w

Boswell, William, printer, 23w near Pen av

Boswell, Barbara, confectioner, btw 9 and 10w and E & Fn
opposite Catholic church

Boswell, Clement. carpenter, Os btw 1 and $\frac{1}{2}$e

Bosworth, J. blacksmith, e side 13w btw E and Fn

Boteler, Charles, police officer, 5w opposite city hall

Boteler, John D gunsmith, n side Pen av btw 3 and $4\frac{1}{2}$w; dw
5w opposite city hall

Bowen, Mrs. M widow, ladies' dress maker and milliner,
n side Pen av btw 9 and 10w

Bowen, James, constable, n side Ns btw 2 and 3e

Bowen, John, guard at the jail, 5w btw F and Gn

Bowen, Thomas, carter, n w corner N Jer av and Ls

Bowen, Doran, laborer, Ls btw 4 and 5e N Yard

Boyd, John, saddler, btw 9 and 10w and E and Fn

Boyd, Richard M. clk in 2d auditor's office; dw Union Tavern, Georgetown

Boyle, John, clk navy department; dw "Retirement," near
university sqnare

Bradley, Abraham, 1st assistant post master general; dw
Georgetown

Bradley, Phineas, 2d   ditto   dw
in the country, 2 miles n e of gen post office

Bradley, P. J. clk in gen post office; dw same

Bradley, William A. president of the Patriotic Bank; dw s w corner 7w and Dn

Bradley, Joseph S. attorney at law, n side Cn btw 6 and 7w

Bradley, Alexander, brushmaker, Fn btw 12 and 13w

Bradley, Robert, carpenter, 10 buildings, N Jer av

Bradley, Mrs. 10s near Eastern Branch, N Yard

Bradford, Joseph, laborer, Gs btw 8 and 9e N Yard

Bradburn, Peter, stonecutter, s w corner As and 2e Cap Hill

Brady, John, laborer, Ks btw 10 and 11e N Yard

Braddock, John, ropemaker, 7e btw F and Gs N Yard

Brannan, John, (firm of Bartow and Brannan, booksellers and stationers) n side Pen av btw 9 and 10w; dw s w corner of Lou av and 6w

Brannan, John, mess pension office; dw Hn btw 18 and 19w

Brashears, Noah, teacher, Pen av btw 17 and 18w

Brawner, Mr. carter, Ls btw 8 and 9e N Yard

Brent, Daniel, chf clk in secretary of state's office; dw at Mrs. Digges' Del av btw B and Cn Cap Hill

Brent, William, clk circuit court, Del av btw B and Cn Cap Hill

Brereton, John A. asst surgeon U. S. army, dw N York av near Col. Tayloe's

Brereton, Samuel, grocer, 15w btw H and In

Brearly, Col. David, Es btw 6 and 7e

Briggs, Samuel, blacksmith, 8e btw I and Ks N Yard

Brightwell, John, asst clk in clk's office county court, s w corner Cn and 2e Cap Hill

Brightwell, James, rigger, Ls btw 6 and 7e N Yard

Brightwell, John L sexton eastern burial ground; dw Md av near the toll gate

Briscoe, Richard S. clk 1st comptroller's office; dw In near western market

Bronaugh, Jeremiah W. clk 1st auditor's office; dw Congress st btw Beall and West sts, Georgetown

Brooke, Edmund, clk pension office; dw Georgetown

Brooke, Walter T. wine and liquor store, n side Pen av 2d
door east National hotel

Brook, Samuel, ch clk treasurer's office; dw 19w btw G & Hn

Brook, G. Washington, carpenter, btw 4½ and Union st
Greenleaf's Point

Brooks, Francis, grocer, corner 5w and Fn

Brooks, Towerhill, Ls btw 4 and 5e N Yard

Brooks, James, laborer, s e corner 5w and En

Brooks, Jerry, (col man) 4½ near Greenleaf's Point

Brooks, Richard, (col man) messenger to Com. Tingey, 7e
btw G and Is N Yard

Brooks, Clement, (col man) laborer, 15w btw G and Hn

Brouillot, Joseph, cutler, s side Fn btw 13 and 14w

Brown, Daniel, clk pension office; dw Gn btw 18 and 19w

Brown, Rev. O. B. clk gen post office; dw En btw 8 and 9w

Browne, William, clk dept of state; dw 18w near In

Brown, Jesse, proprietor Indian Queen hotel, n side Pen
av btw 6 and 7w

Brown, Robert, foreman stonecutter at the Capitol; dw As
fronting Capitol square

Brown, William, tavern, 6w opposite National hotel

Brown, Ann, widow, 5w near Fn

Brown, Robert, n w corner 9w and Fn

Brown, John, livery stable, Cn btw 4½ and 6w; dw btw C
and Dn

Brown, Christopher, laborer, N Jer av btw D and Es

Brown, Nancy, widow, 3e btw M and Ns

Brown, William, laborer, s w corner 7e and Ms N Yard

Brown, Richard, 26w near Georgetown lower bridge

Brown, Mr. shipcarpenter, 7e near N Yard

Brown, Charles B. shoemaker, n w corner Pen av and 11w

Brown, Richard, carpenter, Geo av btw 11 and 12e N Yd

Brown, Peter, Is near 3e

Brown, James, (col man) waiter and whitewasher, near and
north of Capitol

Browning, Greenbury, near 2d Presbyterian church

Brokenborough, Julia, (col woman) washerwoman, s w corner Fn and 22w

Brush, Mary, widow, w side 11e btw Pen av and En

Bryant, James R. M. clk gen land office; dw Prospect farm, north of the Capitol, near northern boundary of the city

Bryan, Elizabeth, widow, 8e opposite marine barracks

Bryan, Mary, widow, grocery, 11e btw L and Ms N Yard

Bryan, Joseph, carpenter, 10w btw F and Gn

Buchanan, Charles, doorkeeper and asst messenger dept of state; dw 12w near In

Buchly, Christian, confectioner, s side Pen av btw 9 & 10w

Buckner, David, 2e near Eastern branch

Buckner, Mr. 6 buildings, Pen av

Buckingham, Caleb, white and lock smith, s side Pen av btw 9 and 10w

Bulfinch, Charles, architect of the Capitol and Penitentiary; dw e side 6w btw D and En

Bull, John, (col man) barber, A s. fronting Capitol square

Bunce, James, blacksmith, Is btw 6 and 7e N Yard

Bunthron, John, stonecutter, 2w btw F and Gn

Burch, Benjamin, doorkeeper House of Representatives, dw n side East Cap st near market, Capitol Hill

Burch, Samuel, ch clk in office of clk of H. of Representatives; dw N Jer av near In

Burch, Thomas, wood measurer, Hn btw 5 and 6w

Burch, Richard, bricklayer, s side Fn opp Catholic church

Burdick, Henry, coachmaker, corner Pen av and 3w

Burdine, Reuben, clk ordnance dept; dw next door east of Unitarian church

Burdine, William, carpenter, Ks btw 10 and 11e N Yard

Burford, Rosetta, widow, grocery, opp market, N Yard

Burgess, Richard, clk 3d auditor's office; dw Georgetown

Burgess, Benjamin, near navy magazine, above Eastern br upper bridge

Burkitt, William, cabinet maker, s side Fn btw 6 and 7w

Burke, John, clk first comptroller's office; dw En btw 13 and 14w

Burk, Francis, printer, Hn near corner 7w

Burnett, Charles, carpenter, Union st Greenleaf's Point

Burnitt, Richard, clk 4th auditor's office; dw at Peck's, s e corner Pen av and 15w

Burns, Benjamin, merchant tailor, s side Pen av opposite Brown's hotel

Burns, Theresa, widow, Fn opposite Catholic church

Burns, Charles, tavern, e side 7w btw G and Hn

Burrowes, John, shoemaker, w side 10w near Pen av

Bury, James, foreman blacksmith at Navy Yard; dw Is btw 6 and 7e, N Yard

Burch, Alexander, cabinet maker, Fn btw 7 and 8e

Burch, R. carpenter, n side Fn btw 6 and 9w

Bushey, George, carpenter, w side 12w btw F and Gn

Bush, Ann, (col woman) Fn btw 21 and 22w

Butler, Julia, widow, N Jer av btw B and Cs Cap Hill

Butler, Thomas, blacksmith, 5e near Eastern branch

Butler, Abraham, tavern, n side Fn btw 13 and 14w

Butler, Mr. carpenter, s side En btw 9 and 10w

Butler, J. B. (col man) carpenter, 11w btw H and In

Butler, Jarrett, (col man) oyster house, 15w near Pen av

Byrne, Christopher, printer, s e corner 10w and Pen av

Byrne, Maria, milliner,   ditto

C.

CAHOON, MARGARET, s w corner Ls and 9c N Yard

Caldwell, Josiah F. clk gen post office; dw Md av near Potomac bridge

Callahan, Patrick, laborer, Cs btw 7 and 8e N Yard

Callan, Nicholas, grocer, s side Fn btw 14 and 15w

Callan, Peter, cabinet maker, s side Fn btw 13 and 14w

Camalier, Vincent, joiner, 6e btw K and Ls N Yard

Campbell, Rev. John, 1u btw 17 and 18w
Campbell, Elizabeth, widow, e side 1u btw D and Eu
Campbell, John, laborer, Vir av btw 6 and 7w
Campbell, Mr. laborer, 26w btw 1 and Kn
Cana, Mary Ann, widow, corner Pen av and Cn
Cannon, Abel, blacksmith, Ks btw 13 and 14e, N Yard
Cannon, Patrick, laborer, Geo av btw 11 and 12e N Yard
Capelano, Antonio, sculptor at the Capitol, N. Jer av btw
    B and Cs Cap Hill
Carbery, Thomas, collector of the port of Washington; dw
    17w near the river
Carbery, James, Vir av btw 3 and 4e
Carroll, Daniel, of Duddington, south of Es btw 1 and 2e
Carroll, Daniel, grocer, s w corner Pen av and 6w
Carroll, Daniel, laborer. As btw 1 and 2e Cap Hill
Carroll, Michael, brass founder, btw 9 and 10e opp N Yard
Carlisle, Mrs. boarding house, s side Pen av btw 4½ and 6w
Carman, William, painter, 1e btw A and Bs Cap Hill
Carr, Overton, asst doorkeeper H. of Representatives; dw
    w side N Jer av btw B and Cs Cap Hill
Carothers, John, stone mason, corner Pen av and 6w
Carothers, Andrew, printer, s w corner 13w and Pen av
Carter, Daniel, merchant tailor, n side Pen av btw 4½ & 6w
Carter, Samuel, stonecutter, Pen av btw 1 and 2e Cap Hill
Carter, Capt. John, brickmaker, Ps Greenleaf's Point
Carter, V. dry goods' store, Pen av opp centre market
Carusi, G. proprietor Washington assembly rooms, corner
    Cn and 11w
Carusi, Nathaniel, professor of music; dw   ditto
Carusi, Samuel,   ditto   ditto
Carusi, Lewis, teacher of dancing,   ditto
Carnes, George, (col man) blacksmith, 4e btw K and Ls
Cassin, James, clk 4th auditor's office; dw Georgetown
Castine, Edward, farmer, Ls btw 2 and 3e
Cassady, Nicholas, shoemaker, 8e opp marine barracks

Catalani, Salvadore, sailing master at navy yard; dw Isbtw 7 and 8e N Yard

Catalani, Antonio, carpenter, 7e btw F and Gs N Yard

Caton, Michael, printer, s side En btw 6 and 7w

Caton, Edward, printer, 3w btw Pen av and Cn

Caton, George W. tailor, e side 9w btw D and En

Causin, Nathaniel P., M. D. north side Pen av near 14w

Cavanaugh, Michael, shoemaker, s side En btw 12 and 13w

Cazenove, Mrs. widow, 14w near the Washington bridge

Chaney, Elijah, grocer, s w corner Fn and 13w

Chaney, Rignul, grocer, 7w btw F and Gn

Chaney, Thomas, painter, An btw 2 and 3e Cap Hill

Charlton, Ralph, grocer, s side Pen av btw 9 and 10w

Chambers, Benjamin, engraver, die sinker, and copper plate printer, s side Pen av btw 9 and 10w

Chase, John, grocer, s w corner Ns and 3w

Chalmers, John, magistrate, Lou av near 7w; dw Vir av btw 3 and 4e

Chapman, John, bricklayer, w side 10w btw G and Hn

Charles, Elizabeth, boarding house, 12w btw C and Dn

Chell, Charles, shoemaker, n side Fn btw 13 and 14w

Cheshire, Archibald, Md av near Washington bridge

Chester, Samuel, boot and shoemaker, Lou av btw 7 and 8w

Childs, Samuel, wood merchant, s e corner Md av and Es near Bradley's wharf

Church, Joseph, laborer, s side Md av btw 3 and 4½w

Clay, Henry, secretary of state; dw 17w corner Hn

Clagett, Darius, (firm of Clagett and Washington) 11w btw F and Gn

Clagett and Washington, dry goods' store, n e corner Pen av and 11w

Clarke, M. St. Clair, clk H. of Representatives; dw n e corner Cn and 4½w

Clark and Millard, dry goods' store, Pen av btw 8 and 9w

Clark, Sarah Ann, widow, e side 12w btw Pen av & En

3

Clark and Orme, dry goods' store, n side Pen av btw 6 & 7w
Clark, John F. druggist,   ditto
Clark, Daniel, gardener, 26 w btw I and Kn
Clark, Joseph S. merchant tailor, (firm of Clark and Orme)
  opposite Brown's hotel, Pen av
Clark, Walter, shoe store, s side Pen av near centre m'kt
Clark, Isaac, hat and shoe store—agent for Union Trans-
  portation Line. s side Pen av near centre market
Clark, Eliza, widow, n side Fn btw 14 and 15w
Clark, Edward W. n w corner Ls and 7e N Yard
Clark, Samuel, cupper and leecher, 2 doors west Mansion
  hotel, Pen av
Clark, Robert, joiner, Ls btw 8 and 9e N Yard
Clark, Robert, magistrate, office s e corner Vir av and 8e
  dw 7e btw Vir av and Is N Yard
Clements, Bennet, clk 3d auditor's office; dw Georgetown
Clements, Mrs. 10 buildings, N Jer av
Clements, A. chairmaker, s side Pen av btw 12 and 13w
Clements, Mary Ann, midwife, 11w near corner Hn
Clements, Albin, 5w near Fn
Clements, Charles A. Mn btw 19 and 20w
Clephane, Lewis, portrait painter, Gn btw 7 and 8w
Clephane, James, printer,   ditto
Clifton, Miss Frances, n w corner 6e and Fs
Clokey, Samuel, carpenter, s side Gn btw 12 and 13w
Clubb, Lewis, fife major marine band; dw Gs btw 6 and 7e
Coad, John, cabinet maker, n side Cn btw 10 and 11w
Coburn, John, grocer, Fn next to bank of Metropolis
Cochrane, Anna, n side Fn btw 13 and 14w
Cochran, George, printer, 5w near Fn
Coltman, William, bricklayer, Dn btw 12 and 13w
Coltman, Charles L. bricklayer, and commissioner 2d ward,
  Dn btw 12 and 13w
Collard, George, carpenter, 4e near Eastern branch
Collard, Elizabeth, widow,   ditto

Collins, Joseph S. clk gen land office, dw east end of Gay street, Georgetown

Collins, Dr. S. In btw 18 and 19w

Collins, Tillinghast, printer, s side En btw 6 and 7w

Collins, Philip, printer, ditto

Collins, George, boatswain's mate at Navy Yard

Collins, Edward, laborer, 13½w btw C and Ds

Collison, Joseph, tailor, 7w near G 1

Collinwood, Andrew, butcher, In btw 20 and 21w

Collinwood, John, weaver, ditto

Coleman, Michael, shoemaker, 13½w btw C and Ds.

Cole, Richard, blockmaker, 10e opposite Navy Yard

Columbus, Charles, shoemaker, n side Pen av btw 4½ and 6w dw 4½w opposite Masonic hall

Colston, Joseph, (col man) hackman, As btw 1 and 2e Capitol Hill

Compton, John S. clk 3d auditor's office; dw N Yk av btw 17 and 18w

Connell, John, messenger treasury dept; Hn near St John's church

Connor, Thomas, blacksmith, 23w near Pen av

Connor, John, carpenter, Vir av btw 4 and 5e

Coninx, M. confectioner, n side Pen av btw 12 and 13w

Cook, Sarah, widow, milliner, Hn near Pen av

Cook, Mary, widow, e side 6w near the Unitarian church

Cook, John, carpenter, 11e btw I and Kn N Yard

Cook, Martha, widow, 3w near Gn

Cookendorffer, Thomas, proprietor Baltimore stages, (old line) office next Indian Queen hotel; dw e side 9w near Pen avenue

Coombe, Griffith, lumber merchant, 3e near Eastern branch

Cooper, jun. William, printer, w side 9w btw D and En

Cooper, Isaac, gilder, s side Pen av btw 13 and 13½w

Cooper, Joseph, wheelwright, In btw 20 and 21w

Cooper, Mary, (col. woman) As btw 1 and 2e Cap Hill

Coote, Clement T. brewer, e side N Jer av near E branch

Corran, Morgan, ditcher, w side 9w btw D and En

Costigan, Eliza, widow, grocery, Ls btw 6 and 7e N Yard

Costen, William, (col. man) A s. fronting Capitol square

Cottringer, Mrs. B. boarding house, w side 13w btw E & Fn

Cottringer, William, clk navy dept dw　　　ditto

Cotter, Martha, e side 10w btw E and Fn

Courtenay, Lieut. Edward H. clk engineer department; dw
　Georgetown

Coumbs, Henry, grocer, Bn btw 6 and 7w

Coumb, Rachel, corner 13½w and Cn

Courtwright, Margaret, widow, Ms btw N Jer av and 1e

Cox, Richard S. attorney at law, Cn east of city hall

Cox, William, wine store, s side Pen av opp Mansion hotel

Cox, Mary, widow, opposite Navy Yard market

Coyle, Matilda, widow, boarding house, near Pen av btw
　11 and 12w

Coyle, Andrew, ch clk gen post office, dw s side Pen av
　btw 6 and 7w

Coyle, John, clk 1st aud's office; dw Bs near N Jer av Cap Hill

Coyle, jr. John,　ditto　　　　　　　ditto

Cozens, Charlotte, widow, s side Pen av btw 21 and 22w

Cranch, William, chief justice circuit court, Del av btw B
　and Cn Cap Hill

Cramer, Jacob, blacksmith, Union st Greenleaf's Point

Crandall, George, carpenter, Gn btw 11 and 12w

Crandle, James, shoemaker, w side 5e near Eastern Branch

Craven, John, clk 4th auditor's office; dw 19w near Baptist
　church

Craven, Philip, coppersmith, w side 7e btw K & Ls N Yard

Craig, Ann Maria, Is near N Jer av

Cressell, Thomas, bookbinder, w side 8w btw G and Hn

Cripps, William M'L. cabinet maker, w side 11w btw Pen
　av and En; dw nearly opposite

Criddle, Jonathan, millwright, 7e btw G and Is N Yard

Crowley, Margaret, widow, cook shop, n side Pen av btw
　2 and 3w

Crowley, Patrick, printer, n w corner 6w and Fn
Crook, Nancy, Ls near Eastern Branch
Croker, Samuel (col. man) seaman, 6w btw E and Fn
Cromwell, Jesse, shoemaker, n side Pen av btw 9 and 10w
Cross. Major T. clk qr master general's office; dw 15w near
bank Metropolis
Cross, Thomas, brickmaker, Ls btw 4 and 5e N Yard
Cross. George, dw   ditto
Cross, Eli, dw   ditto
Cross Francis, carter, 4e btw K and Ls N Yard
Cross, Mary Ann, widow, w side N Jer av btw I and Ks
Crossen, William, teacher at the Catholic seminary
Crossfield, Jehiel, printer, at Mrs. Lanphier's, s side Pen
av btw 9 and 10w
Crosen, Samuel, brickmaker, Vir av near old tanyard
Crown, Jeremiah, laborer, Kn btw 18 and 19w
Cruttenden, Harvey, brickmaker, e side N Jer av btw B & Cs
Cruzen, Jacob, gunsmith, 7e btw L and Ms N Yard
Cull, John, stonecutter, East Cap st btw 2 and 3e Cap Hill
Cummerfod, Sarah, tavern, Ms btw 4½ and 6w Greenleaf's
Point
Cumberland, John, carpenter, btw 21 & 22w near the river
Cummins, Christopher, tailor, n side Pen av btw 13 and 14w;
dw s side Fn btw 13 and 14w
Cunningham, Margaret, widow, corner 14w and Cn
Curly, James, teacher in the Catholic seminary
Curry, Benjamin, laborer, 12w btw C and Dn
Cutbush, Edward, surgeon U. States' navy, n side Pen av
near 14w
Cutting, John B. clk war department; dw n side Fn btw 13
and 14w
Cutts, Richard 2d comptroller; dw Hn near St. John's church
Cuvillier, musician in marine band; dw 19e btw F and Gs
Navy Yard
3*

D.

DAGGETT, Mr. blacksmith, Ns btw 4½ and Union st Green-leaf's Point

Danford, John, baker and grocer, opp Navy Yard market

Darnes, Hanson, laborer, Is btw 3 and 4e

Dashiel, Thomas R. clk treasurer's office; dw corner In & 18w

Dashiell, George W. clk treasurer's office; dw N York av btw 17 and 18w

Datcher, Francis, (col. man) messenger, In btw 15 and 16w

Davidson, James, clk 3d auditor's office ; dw Fn near 13w

Davidson, John, s e corner Gn and 27w, near Georgetown

Davidson, Nelson, coachmaker, corner Pen av and 13½w

Davis, Gideon, clk in sec'y of war's office; dw Georgetown

Davis, John, boarding house, n side Cn btw 4½ and 6w

Davis, Rev. John, Gn next to Methodist church

Davis, James, tailor, w side 8w btw G and Hn

Davis, David, tailor, n side Pen av btw 17 and 18w

Davis, of Abel, John, master plumber at the Navy Yard; dw Is btw 10 and 11e N Yard

Davis, Charles, messenger 1st auditor's office; dw n side En btw 9 and 10w

Davis, William A. bookseller and stationer, next door west of the Indian Queen hotel, Penn avenue

Davis, George, grocer, Md av near Washington bridge

Davis, George P. grocer, s side Pen av btw 12 and 13w

Davis, Catharine, milliner, n side Pen av btw 3 and 4½w

Davis, Eli, shoemaker, n side Fn btw 6 and 7w

Davis, Sarah, widow, s side East Cap st btw 3 and 4e

Davis, Robert, (col. man) laborer, btw 13 and 14w near Gn

Dawson, Ann, widow, 2w btw F and Gn

Dawson, Aaron, hatter, 8w corner Gn

Dawson, Henrietta, widow, Is btw 4 and 5e N Yard

Dawes, Henry, shoemaker, Lou av near Penn av btw 8 & 9w

Day, Sarah, n side Fn btw 8 and 9w

De Krafft, Edward, printer and bookbinder, n e corner 7w
and Lou av; dw e side 7w btw E and Fn

De Krafft, Frederick Cornelius, clk in Patriotic bank, and
city surveyor; dw s side En btw 9 and 10w

Delaplaine, Githens, 2e near Md av Cap Hill

Delano, Judah, printer, s side Fn btw 6 and 7w

Delany, Patrick, tavern, s side Fn btw 13 and 14w

Delany, George, coachmaker; dw at Appler's, Fountain Inn

Delany, Adams, (col. man) carter, Md av btw 1 and 2w

Deming, William, clk gen post office; dw n side Dn btw
6 and 7w

Deneale, James C. 11e near bridge, N Yard

Denham, Mrs. widow, tailoress, 14w near Pen av

Dennison, John, bricklayer, e side 10w btw D and En

Denoon, Elizabeth, widow, w side N Jer av btw I and Ks

Dent, Susan (col. woman) washerwoman, n w corner 13w
and Cs

Derrick, William S. clk in department of state; dw Fn btw
12 and 13w

Deschard, Charles, blacksmith, 20 buildings, South Cap st

Detro, Thomas, (col. man) stone mason, s e corner Gn & 6w

Devlin, John, sergeant marines, Is btw 12 and 13e N Yard

Devaughn, Mrs. spinster, Gn near 5w

Dewees, William, clk 5th audit's office; dw 13w btw F & Gn

Dewdney, John, grocer, corner 23w and Pen av

Dickins, Asbury, clk in secretary treasury's office; dw Fn
near corner 13w

Digges, Mrs. widow, Del av btw B and Cn Capitol Hill

Digges, James, ship carpenter, Gs btw 6 and 7e N Yard

Digges, William, brickmaker, 20w btw E and Fn

Digges, Anthony, (col. man) laborer, A s. fronting Capitol
square

Dines, Henny, (col woman) Gn btw 6 and 7w

Ditty, Samuel, merchant tailor, n side Pen av btw 9 and
10w; dw n side Dn btw 10 and 11w

Dix, Sophia, widow, n side Fn btw 13 and 14w

Dix, John, merchant tailor, nearly opposite Indian Queen hotel, Pen av

Dixon, Elizabeth, widow, gardener, e side 1e btw B and Cn Capitol Hill

Dixon, Jacob, grocery, s w corner Fn and 11w

Dodds, James, stonecutter, Pen av near 15w

Dodson, William, caulker, Is near 3e

Donoho, Thomas, clk in office National Intelligencer; dw n w corner Dn and 9w

Donoho, Patrick, s e corner Cs and 13½w

Donohoo, John A. grocer, s e corner 7w and Gn

Donohoo, Mary, grocery, n e corner 7w and Gn

Donohue, John, grocery and shoe store, n side Pen av btw 10 and 11w

Dorney, William W. laborer, 10e opposite N Yard

Dorrett, J. Wilkes, laborer, 10 buildings, N Jer av

Dorset, Fielder R. carpenter, Es btw 9 and 10w

Dorsey, James, grocer, s e corner E. Cap st & 1e Cap Hill

Dougherty, Nathaniel, shoemaker, 10e btw G & Hs N Yard

Dougherty, William, Ls btw 4 and 5e N Yard

Dougherty, James, tavernkeeper, s side Fn btw 13 and 14w

Douglass, Elizabeth, widow, Mn near Georgetown up bridge

Douglass, Miss E. dress and pelisse maker, 19w btw Pen av and Hn

Douglass, Betsey, washerwoman, near Georgetown lower bridge

Douglass, Elizabeth, widow, n side East Cap st btw 1 and 2e Capitol Hill

Douglass, William, carpenter, s side Pen av btw 9 and 10w

Dove, Marmaduke, sailing master U. States' navy, 11e one door below Ks N Yard

Dove, Thos. mess'r 3d aud's office; dw Ver av btw H & In

Dove, Joseph, n side Fn btw 11 and 12w

Dover, James, (col. man) laborer, s side East Capitol st btw 3 and 4e Cap Hill

Dowson, Alfred R. boarding house, A n. fronting Cap square

Dowling, William, tavernkeeper, s side Fn btw 13 and 14w

Dowling, Thomas, printer, e side 10w btw D and En

Downes, Mary, spinster, Hn btw 9 and 10w

Doyle, Martin, canal wharf, Eastern branch

Drew, Solomon, tailor, 7w btw Louisana av and Dn; agent for the Howard Institution, s side Pen av op centre market

Druet, James, tailor, s side Pen av btw 19 and 20w

Drummond, John C. corner Ms and 6w

Drummond, Richard H. carpenter, Vir av btw 6 and 7w

Drummond, William S. carpenter, Cn btw 3 and 4½w

Drury, Samuel, cabinet maker, Pen av btw 21 and 22w

Duckworth, George, s w corner 7w and Ls N Yard

Duckworth, George, jun. grocer, next to s w corner Ls and 7e N Yard

Duff, John, (col. man) corner N York av and 21w

Duncan, William, printer, n w corner En and 12w

Duncan, Mary, boarding house, 6w near En

Dunning, John, butcher, n w corner Ns and N Jer av

Dungan, Thomas, clk secretary of war's office; dw Fn btw 12 and 13w

Dunn, John Oswald, sergeant-at-arms Ho. of Representatives; dw 1e btw B and Cn Capitol Hill

Dunn, James C. printer, s side Kn near Georgetown lower bridge

Dunn, John, builder, Is btw 6 and 7e N Yard

Durden, Charles, (col. man) laborer, Gn btw 2 and 3w

Duvall, Washington, blockmaker, 11e near bridge N Yard

Dwyer, Thomas, stonecutter, n side East Cap st btw 2 and 3c Capitol Hill

Dyer, Thomas, clk in gen post office; dw En opp gen post office

Dyer, John R. clk in gen post office; dw 7w btw I and Kn

Dyer, Edward, clk city post office; dw s e corner 8w and En

Dyer, William B. carpenter, corner Dn and 14w

E.

EAKIN, JAMES, ch clk 2d auditor's office; dw Gadsby's National hotel

Earle, Robert, hack driver, Hn btw 20 and 21w

Earp, James, shoemaker, 13w btw C and Dn

Easton, David, clk 5th auditor's office; dw n w corner 19w and In

Easby, William, master boat builder at navy yard; dw E's btw 9 and 10e

Easter, John, w side 10w btw D and En

Eaton, David, boatswain at navy yard; dw in the yard

Eaton, Nathaniel, messenger navy department; dw 13w near Fn

Ebbins Phœbe, (col. woman) Pen av btw 19 and 20w

Eckloff, Christian, merchant tailor, n side Pen av btw 12 and 13w

Eckhart, Henry, butcher, near the glass house

Eckhart, John,   ditto   ditto

Edelin, Mrs. widow, w side 6w btw D and En

Edeline, Stanislaus, laborer, Ms btw 9 and 10e N Yard

Edmonston, Nathan, carpenter, w side 6w btw D and En

Edmonston, Mary, widow, w side 6w btw D and En

Edmonston, Sarah, En btw 9 and 10w

Edwards, James L. ch clk pension office; dw 17w btw H and I n. near St. John's church

Edwards, James, clk in secretary of war's office; dw Gn btw 18 and 19w west of the war office

Elden, John, shoemaker, corner Cn and 11w

Elder, William, grocer, 8e opp marine barracks, N Yard

Elgar, Joseph, commissioner public buildings; dw w side 14w btw F and Gn

Elkins, Jeremiah, attorney at law, s side Pen av btw 9 & 10w

Eliot, William G. clk gen post office; dw Lou av btw 6 & 7w

Eliot, Mary, widow, 4½w btw N and Os Greenleafs Point

Elliot. William, 1st clk in patent office; dw North Capitol street, near the Capitol

Elliott, Richard, asst. navy commissioners' office; dw Kn btw 23 and 24w

Elliot, Elizabeth, widow, w side 10w btw D and En

Elliot, Jonathan, printer, n side Pen av btw 3 and 4½w

Elliot, S. A. printer; office 11w btw Pen av and Cn; dw at Mrs. M'Cauley's, Pen av btw 10 and 11w

Ellison, William C clk in gen post office; at C. K. Gardner's, Capitol Hill

Ellison, Mr. carpenter, Ns btw 3 and 4½w

Ellis, Robert, clk 2d auditor's office; dw Gn btw 21 & 22w

Ellis, John, tallow chandler, s w corner Fn and 9w

Ellis, John, carpenter. 3w near Pen avenue

Ellis, Leonard, laborer, N York av btw 21 and 22w

Ellis, William B. principal engineer steam engine in navy yard, Georgia av op N Yard

Elzey, Henrietta, s w corner 18w and Gn

Emack, William, dry goods' and grocery store, s side East Capitol st opposite market, Cap Hill

Emack, A. G. grocer, 7w btw F and Gn

Embree, Daniel, inspector of flour, s w-corner 7w and In

Emery, Paul, coachmaker, 13w btw Pen av and Dn

English, John C. & Co. hardware store, s side Pen av btw 9 and 10w

Ennis, Gregory, tavernkeeper, n side Pen av btw 1 and 2e

Ennis, Philip, 6w btw E and Fn

Eno, Richard, s side Kn near Georgetown lower bridge

Enslow, James, blacksmith, Fs btw 7 and 8e

Ensey, William, tailor, n side Ls btw 7 and 8e N Yard

Essex, Deborah, widow, opposite Navy Yard market

Essex, Josiah, carpenter, n side Hn btw 6 and 7w

Este, John, bookbinder and stationer, s side Pen av btw 9 and 10w

Evans, Philip, ship carpenter, 10e btw K and Ls N Yard

Evans, sen. Jesse, corner Ks and 11e N Yard

Evans, Jesse, ship carpenter, Ks btw 10 and 11e N Yard

Evans, Travers, carter, Vir av btw 7 and 8e N Yard

Evans, William, 7e btw L and Ms N Yard

Evans, John, bricklayer, Vir av btw 6 and 7w

Evans, Joseph, bricklayer, As btw 1 and 2e Capitol Hill

Evans, George, laborer, Bs btw 1e and N Jer av Cap Hill

Evans, Walter, grocery, Ks btw 10 and 11e N Yard

Evans, Walter, 6e btw G and Is N Yard

Evans, William, laborer, corner Is and 4e

Evans, John, bricklayer, Vir av btw 6 and 7e N Yard

Evans, Davis, (col. man) 12w near Hn

Evans, David, (col. man) brickmaker, 15w corner Ls

Ewell James, M. D. corner A s. and 1e fronting the Capitol
square, Capitol Hill

F.

Fadeuilhe, William, upholsterer, n w corner Dn and 10w

Fagan, Joseph, turner, dw btw En and Pen av

Fagan, Nicholas, carpenter, 11w btw E and Fn

Fales, Nathan W. grocer, n e corner Pen av and 10w; dw
e side 10w btw D and En

Farlan, John, w side 7w btw D and Es

Farrow, John, filer, 11e btw K and Ls N Yard

Fawcett, Lyle B. clk engineer department; dw Georgetown

Fearson, Samuel, merchant, near Georgetown lower bridge

Fearson, Joseph N merchant, n w corner Kn and 27w

Fendall, Mary, widow, boarding house, s side Fn btw 12
and 13w

Fendall, Philip Richard, clk secretary of state's office

Fendall, Ferrel, e side N Jer av btw K and Ls

Fenwick, Richard, porter at bank of Metropolis; dw s side
Fn btw 10 and 11w

Fenwick, Washington, bricklayer, s side Hn btw 6 and 7w

Fenner, J. P. clk in war department

Fenwick, Robert W. messenger in patent office; dw s w corner Fn and 8w

Ferria, Francis, razor grinder, w side 12w near En

Ferrel, Joseph, laborer, 7e btw L and Ms

Fergusson, Enos D. grocer, s side Pen av btw 4½ and 6w

Field, Maurice, tailor, corner 14w and Pen av

Fillebrown, Thomas, clk in secretary navy's office; dw Gn near 21w

Finley, James I s. near N Jer av

Fisher, Lydia, widow, w side 3e btw M and Ns

Fitton, Thomas, ship carpenter, near the bridge, N Yard

Fitzpatrick, John, joiner at navy yard; dw opposite marine barracks

Fitzhugh, Samuel, clk gen post office; dw Md avenue, near Washington bridge

Flanigan, Michael, stonemason, n side Dn btw 6 and 7w

Fletcher, Noah, clk in clk's office H. of Representatives; dw n side En btw 6 and 7w

Fletcher, William, ship carpenter; 28w near Georgetown lower bridge

Flemming, John, laborer, A s. fronting Capitol square

Fleury, Eliza, widow, 14w btw Pen av and Fn

Fleet, Thomas, (col.) hairdresser, 6w opp National hotel

Follinsby, Joseph, carpenter, 2e btw A n. and East Cap st Capitol Hill

Foley, Adolphus, stonecutter, Bn btw 1 and 2e Capitol hill

Force, Peter, proprietor National Journal, s w corner 11w and Pen av; dw e side 10w btw D and En

Ford, Sarah, milliner, s side Pen av btw 9 and 10w

Forrest Jane, widow, 13w near corner Hn

Forrest, Henry, clk 4th auditor's office; dw   ditto

Forrest, Samuel,   ditto   ditto

Forrest, Joseph, clk to commissioners Florida treaty; dw corner Fn and 20w

4

Forrest, Richard, clk secretary state's office; dw Fn near 14w

Forrest, Andrew, alderman for 6th ward; n w corner Ks and 8e N Yard

Forrest, Alexander, sergeant major marine corps, at the barracks, N Yard

Forman, David, stonecutter, btw B and Cn and 1 and 2e Capitol Hill

Foster, Edward, asst. draughtsman to naval constructor; dw 8e opposite marine barracks, N Yard

Fottrell, Jacob, w side 10w btw Pen av and Fn

Fowler, Col. Benjamin, clk engineer dep't: dw Georgetown

Fowler, Charles S. (firm of S. and M. Allen & Co.) dw w side 7w btw E and Fn

Fowler, Abraham, carpenter, Ks btw 6 and 7e N Yard

Fowler, James H. carpenter, 11w btw Md av and Es

Fowler, George, Bn btw 3 and 4e Cap Hill

Fowler, William,   ditto

Fowler, Samuel, Ls btw 7 and 8e N Yard

Fowler, Julia, grocery, n side Pen av btw 3 and 4½w

Foyles, Thomas, butcher, w side 7e near N Yard

Foy, John, superintendent Cap square garden; dw Pen av west of, and near the Capitol

France, John, fancy store, n side Pen av btw 12 and 13w

Frank, Mrs. widow, boarding house, En btw 9 and 10w

Franklin, Stephen P. paper hanger, opp Indian Queen hotel

Franklin, Ann, milliner,   ditto

Franklin, Nicholas, (col. man) caulker, s e corner Ks & 4e

Frankland, Henry William, sailmaker, e side 7e btw Vir av and Is N Yard

Franzoni, Mrs. widow, 4½w opposite new masonic hall

Frazer, John, blacksmith, s e corner 1 s. and 4e

Frazer, Horatio, laborer, 7e near N Yard

Frazier, Patrick, (col. man) near corner Mn and 15w

Freeman, Margaret, widow, boarding house, 7 buildings, Pen avenue

Freeman, John, (col. man) waiter at Gadsby's hotel; dw Kn near 19w

French, Ebenezer, clk secretary of treasury's office; dw west end 6 buildings, Pen av

French, William, bricklayer, A s. btw 1 and 2e Cap Hill

French, William, n e corner 13w and Fn

French, Alexander, shoemaker, 2w btw F and Gn

Frere, James, mess. 2d auditor's office; Hn btw 21 and 22w

Friend, James, baker, corner Ks and 11e N Yard

Fridley, George, tailor, n side Fn btw 6 and 7w

Fronk, Lewis, glass blower, near the glass house

Frost, John T., N Jer av btw B and Cs Cap Hill

Fry, James, carpenter, N Jer av btw C and Ds Cap Hill

Frye, Nathaniel, ch clk paymaster general's office; dw near Georgetown lower bridge

Frye, Robert, fisherman, 7e near N Yard

Furlong, John, coach smith, 13w btw C and Ds

G.

GADSBY, JOHN, proprietor National Hotel, n e corner Pen av and 6w

Gahan, William, shoemaker, n side En btw 6 and 7w

Gaither, Greenbury, watchmaker and silversmith, s side Pen av btw 10 and 11w

Gaither, James, carpenter, Gn btw 21 and 22w

Gales, jun. Joseph, (firm of Gales and Seaton) dw n west corner En and 9w

Gales and Seaton, proprietors National Intelligencer, n w corner 7w and Dn

Gallaudet, P. W. clk reg's office; dw at Col. Nourse's, 15w

Gallagher, Thomas, laborer, 2w btw F and Gn

Galt, James, watchmaker, n side Pen av btw 9 and 10w

Galvin, Dorcas, boarding house, 1e fronting Capitol square, Capitol Hill

Galloway, William, livery stable keeper, 14w btw Dn and Pen av; dw corner 13w and Gn

Gamble, Maj. William, e side N Jer av btw B and Cs Capitol Hill

Gannon, James, 9w btw D and En

Gardner, Charles K. clk general post office, dw N Jer av Capitol Hill

Gardner, Capt. J. L. clk qr master general's office; dw Hn btw 20 and 21w

Gardner, Henry S. clk 2d auditor's office; dw Hn

Gardner, Samuel, dyer, Kn near Georgetown lower bridge

Gardner, David A. n side Gn btw 14 and 15w

Gardiner, John, commissioner 3d ward, Fn btw 9 and 10w

Garner, John, laborer, 10 buildings, N Jer av

Garrick, Martin, 5e near Eastern branch

Gassaway, Hanson, hardware store, n e corner Pen av & 9w

Gates, Robert, grocer, s e corner 10e and Ms N Yard

Geddes, Adam, coppersmith, Geo av btw 9 and 10e N Yard

Gessendeiner, Henry, blacksmith, 7e btw L and Ms N Yard

Getty, Robert, clk 4th auditor's office; dw Fn near 10w

Gibbons, John, carpenter, 8w near Gn

Gibberson, Charles, bricklayer, 4½w btw L and Ms Greenleaf's Point

Gibbs, A. C. merch't, (firm of Gibbs & Coyle,) Pen av near 7w

Gibson, Col. George, commissary general of subsistence; dw e side 14w btw Pen av and Fn

Gibson, Joseph, grocery store, n side Pen av btw 11 and 12w; dw s side Pen av btw 10 and 11w

Gibson, Richard, painter, Mn near Georgetown up. bridge

Gibson, William, boatman, Virginia av btw 6 and 7w

Gibson, John, painter, 11e near the bridge, N Yard

Gibson, jr. John, shipcarpenter, dw ditto

Gideon, Jacob, (firm of Way and Gideon) dw w side 9w btw Pen av and Dn

Gilbert, William, grocer, s e corner Fn and 13w

Gilder, R. lottery office, n side Pen av btw 9 and 10w

Gillin, Jeremiah, laborer, A s. opp Cap square, Cap Hill

Gilliss, Thomas H. ch clk 4th aud's office; dw Fn near 10w

Gilliss, George,   ditto   dw north of St. John's church

Givenny, Bernard, grocer, s side Bs btw 1e and N Jer av Cap Hill

Givens, Thomas, carpenter, Cn btw 11 and 12w

Givens, Eliza, (col. woman) 13w btw C and Dn

Gleason, William, blockmaker at N Yard; dw Ks btw 10 and 11e N Yard

Glover, Mrs widow, e side 10w btw D and En

Glynn, Anthony G. clk pension office; dw Georgetown

Goddard, J. H. tavern, w side 7w btw Dn and Lou av

Goldsborough, Charles W. sec'y to navy commissioners, Gn west of war office

Golden, John, shoemaker, 8w btw D and En

Golden, Ellen, widow, n side Fn btw 7 and 8w

Golden, Richard R. grocer, s w corner Fn and 7w

Gooch, J plasterer, 8e btw L and Ms N Yard

Goodall, Thomas, filer, 9e btw L and Ms N Yard

Gordon, W. A. clk in quarter master general's office; dw 14w btw F and Gn

Gordon, Martha, widow, n w corner Bn and 1e Capitol Hill

Gordon, Mary, widow, sempstress, 13½w btw Pen av and Dn

Gorman, John B. painter, Cn near centre market, dw at Mrs. Arguelles'

Goss, Captain, 20w btw N York av and Fn

Grace, William, teacher at Catholic seminary

Graham, George, commissioner gen land office; dw En btw 20 and 21w

Graham, Mrs A. ladies' corsett and gentlemen's belt maker, Gn btw 18 and 19w

Graham, Araminta, widow, e side 12w btw E and Fn

Grant, George, bricklayer, 4e near Eastern branch.

4*

Grammer, G. C. wine and liquor store, s side Pen av opposite Indian Queen hotel

Granger, William, carpenter, Ms btw 4½ and 6w Greenleaf's Point

Grant, George, shipcarpenter, n side Vir av btw 7 and 8e Navy Yard

Graff, John, (col. man) waiter, s w corner Gn and 6w

Gray, Stephen W. clk gen post office; dw n w corner En and 10w

Gray, Henrietta, (col. woman) e side 8w btw D and En

Gray, Betsey, (col. woman) Gn btw 6 and 7w

Green, John, clk to navy commissioners, Pen av btw 17 and 18w

Green, Duff, proprietor United States' Telegraph, En btw 9 and 10w; dw same

Green, James D. and Co. hatters, 1st door east of Nat. hotel

Green, Elizabeth, grocery, s e corner Fn and 11w

Gregory, James S merchant, n side Pen av. btw 9 and 10w; dw at Mrs. M'Cauley's, btw 10 and 11w Pen av

Grennell, Philip O. joiner, 7e btw K and Ls Navy Yard

Greiner, Eleanor, N Yk av btw 18 and 19w

Gresham, Sterling, clk gen land office; dw High st Georgetown, near intersection of F and 4n

Griffin, Peter, joiner, Ls btw 4 and 5e N Yard

Grouard, George M. printer, office National Intelligencer, corner 7w and Dn

Grouard, Mrs. 9w near corner Fn

Grumble, Sandy, boatman, 28w near Georgetown Pr bridge

Gunnell, James S., M. D. dentist, n side Pen av btw 9 and 10w

Gunnell, William H. druggist, e side N Jer av btw A and Bs; dw n e corner Ds and 6e

Gunton, William, apothecary, n w corner Pen av and 9w

Gunton, Thomas, clk 3d auditor's office; dw ditto

Gurley, Ralph R. agent of colonization society, opposite Mansion hotel, Pen av

Guttschlich, Ernest, proprietor Shakspeare hotel, Louisiana avenue, next to the theatre

H.

HAAG, PERRY, rigger, 10c opposite navy yard

Hacket, Mary, (col. woman) washerwoman, south side Gn near 15w

Hagan, Horatio, joiner, 7c btw K and Ls Navy Yard

Hagner, Peter, 3d auditor, Hn near 13w

Hall, O. S. clk 2d auditor's office; dw at Peck's, s e corner Pen av and 15w

Hall, D. A. attorney at law, 7w btw D and En

Hall, Samuel, dry goods' store, s side Pen av btw 6 and 7w

Hall, Mary Ann, (col. woman) teacher, s side Pen av btw 1 and 2e Cap Hill

Hall, James, (col. man) waiter at treasury department, Hn btw 15 and 16w

Hamilton, Samuel S. clk Indian department; dw n side Pen av btw 9 and 10 w

Hamilton, Mrs. widow, 1c fronting Capitol square

Hamilton, Charles B., M. D n w corner Is and 6w N Yard

Hamilton, Matthew, bricklayer, Cn btw 12 and 13w

Hamilton, Rhode, 26w btw I and Kn

Handy, S. W. hatter, n side Pen av near Indian Queen hotel

Handy, jun Samuel, clk 1st comptroller's office; dw n side Pen av btw 12 and 13w

Handy, James H. clk 4th auditor's office; dw 17w btw H & In

Handy, Edward G. clk to commissioner public buildings, dw e side N Jer av btw B and Cs Cap hill

Handly, James, printer, s side Fn btw 6 and 7w

Handly, John, plasterer, 20w btw Fn and N York av

Handley, Edmond, plasterer,   ditto

Hand, I. W. clk gen post office; Fn btw 11 and 12w

Hanson, Samuel, clk 1st comptroller's office; dw at R. C. Weightman's

Hanson, Grafton D. clk gen post office; dw near marine barracks

Hanson, Isaac K. clk in register's office; dw btw 19 and 20w

Hardy, Richard, teacher in the Catholic seminary

Harper, Nicholas, clk 5th auditor's office; dw Pen av near National hotel

Harper, William, wheelwright, btw 4½ and Union street, Greenleaf's Point

Harper, Joel, shoemaker, round tops, near Georgetown

Harper, William, stonecutter, 3w btw F and Gn

Harrison, Richard, 1st auditor, n w corner In and 13w

Harrison, Benjamin, clk 1st comptroller's office; dw 17w btw IIn and Pen av

Harrison, R. M. carpenter, Vermont av btw H and In

Harrison, Samuel, 11w btw E and Fn

Harrison, James, blacksmith, I s btw 12 and 13e N Yard

Harrison, Richard, laborer, w side 7e btw F and Gs N Yd

Harrington, Miss Maria, w side N Jer av btw K and Ls

Harris, John, bootmaker, e side 7w btw G and IIn

Harris, Charlotte, (col. woman) Kn near Georgetown lower bridge

Harbaugh, Joseph, grocer, w side 7w btw D and En

Harkins, William, painter, s side Fn btw 14 and 15w

Harkness, Samuel, commissioner 1st ward, I n btw 20 & 21w

Hartman, Kitty, near the glass house

Hartman, Catharine, widow, ditto

Harvey, John, Geo av btw 9 and 10e N Yard

Haskell, Joseph, clk gen post office; dw Kn intersection of N York and Massachusetts avenues

Haskell. D. H. teacher, 16w next St. John's church

Hauptman, Daniel, tinman, s side Dn near Pen av and 12w

Haughey, James C. clk qr master general's office; dw Gn near Davidson's wharf

Havener, Thomas, baker, s side Cn btw 4½ and 6w

Hawley, Rev. William, rector of St. John's church; dw N York av opposite 2d Presbyterian church

Haw, John S. clk in register's office; dw Georgetown

Hawkins, Charles, (col. man) near corner 15w and Kn

Hay, Charles, ch clk Secretary navy's office; dw 1st st., Georgetown

Hayre, Francis, grocer, Vir av btw 7 and 8e N Yard

Hazel, Zachariah, tavernkeeper, 2e btw A and Bn Cap Hill

Heffernan, Patrick, laborer, Gn btw 2 and 3w

Hefly, Frederick, tinner, n side Dn btw 10 and 11w

Heighton, John, A s. btw 3 and 4e Cap Hill

Hellen, Johnson, attorney at law, w side 11w near Pen av

Hendley, Richard, tavernkeeper, s e corner 7w and En near gen post office

Henderson, Samuel, Bn near Del av Cap hill

Henderson, Archibald, colonel of marines, at the barracks, Navy Yard

Henderson, Thomas, M. D.; office 11w btw Pen av and Dn

Henry, Joshua, shoemaker, I n. btw 20 and 21w

Hendill, Thomas carpenter, next eastern public school

Henning, Stephen, 11e btw I and Ks N Yard

Hepburn, John, lk in adjt general's office; dw Georgetown

Hepburn, Alice, midwife, Gn btw 7 and 8w

Hepburn, Peter carpenter, 13½w near Washington bridge

Hepburn, Alexander, gardener, e side N Jer av btw B and Cs Capitol Hill

Herbert, Joseph, ship carpenter, w side 7e near navy yard

Herbert, Thomas, proprietor Columbian garden, 27w btw G and Hn

Herbert, Nathaniel, (col. man) porter gen post office; dw 8w near Gn

Hereus, George, carpenter, 11w btw Md av and Fs

Herrington, Richard, constable, n w corner Ks and 11e N Yard

Hewitt, William, city register, office west wing city hall;
 dw 6w opposite Unitarian church

Hewgitt, Joseph, grocer, e side 3e near Eastern branch

Heyer, Miss, boarding house, e side N Jer av btw B and Cs
 Cap Hill

Hickey, Mary, widow, boarding house, e side N Jer av
 btw A and Bs Cap Hill

Hickey, William, clk secretary senate's office; dw same

Hickey, Daniel, bricklayer, A n. btw 1 and 2e Cap Hill

Hickey, Michael, s side Es btw 1e and N. Jer av Cap Hill

Hicks, Robert, painter and glazier, Pen av btw 19 and 20w

Higdon, Gustavus, dry goods' store, s side Ls btw 8 and 9e
 Navy Yard

Higdon, John, e side 12w near Pen av

Higgins, Martin F. n w corner 7w and Gn

Hilleary, Theodore W. cabinet maker, n w corner Fs and 5e

Hill, Henry V. cabinet maker, s side Pen av btw 4½ and 6w

Hilton, Samuel, dry goods' store, e side 8e near N Yard

Hilbus, Jacob, organ builder, s w corner 17w and Hn

Hilyard, Nathan, grocery, corner 14w and Pen av

Hilyard, John, tavern, n w corner 7w and Hn

Hines, Philip, baker, Hn near Pen av

Hines, Frederick, grocer, s w corner Pen av and 18w

Hines, Abraham,   ditto

Hines, C. and M. grocers, s w corner 20w and Pen av

Hines, John, s w corner 7e and Ks N Yard

Hines, Henry, carter, corner Hn and 18w

Hines, Jacob, asst messenger 1st comptroller's office; 1 n
 btw 18 and 19w

Hoban, James, architect, n side Fn btw 14 and 15w

Hobbs, Ann, widow, corner 13½w and Cn

Hoburg, John, upholsterer and paper hanger, s w corner
 Pen av and 9w; dw 13w near Dn

Hodson, Lydia, n side Kn near Georgetown lower bridge

Hodges, Mrs. widow, w side 11w btw E and Fn

Hodgson, John, sailmaker, Ks btw 8 and 9e N Yard

Hodge, William, laborer, 7e btw L and Ms N Yard

Hodges, William, saddler, 1e btw East Cap st and As Cap Hill

Hogan, Thady, Fn opp Catholic church

Holland, Edward, messenger in 5th auditor's office; dw 12w corner Gn

Holiam, Mr. rigger, Ls btw 8 and 9e Navy Yard

Holliday, Thomas, gun smith at navy yard; dw I s btw 7 and 8e & Yard

Holmead, John B. dry goods' store, Louisiana av btw 7 and 8w opposite centre market

Holmead, Anthony, dry goods' store, Lou avenue, opposite centre market; dw e side 4½w near Pen av

Holroy, John, n side I s. btw 10 and 11e N Yard

Holsom, Ebenezer, tavernkeeper, 7w opp centre market

Homans, Benjamin, clk in secr'y navy's office; dw George-town

Homan, Daniel, carpenter, A s btw 1 and 2e Cap Hill

Hooper, Thomas H. laborer, 11w near Carusi's assembly rooms

Hooper, T. laborer, Fn btw 21 and 22w

Hooper, Elizabeth, widow, Ms btw 4½ and 6w Greenleaf's Point

Hoover, Barbara, widow, corner Gn and 9w

Hoover, Michael, butcher,   ditto

Hoover, John, butcher, near N York av and 5w

Hoover, Andrew, bootmaker, n side Pen av btw 20 and 21w opposite 7 buildings

Hoot, Eliza, boarding house, e side 10w btw D and En

Hoote, Naomi, widow, w side 10w btw E and Fn

Hopkins, Evan, hairdresser, Lou av opposite centre market

Hopkins, Solomon, e side N Jer av btw btw K and Ls

Horton, Josiah, agent for proprietors of Baltimore stages (old line) next to Indian Queen hotel

Hornor, Reuben W. hardware merchant, s side Pen av btw
  4½ and 6w

Hornor, Elizabeth, 9e near Vir av Navy Yard

Hosier, James M. grocer, corner Lou av and 7w; dw 11w
  btw Pen av and En

Hoskins, John, baker, 26w near Georgetown upper bridge

Houston, John H. clk 5th auditor's office; dw corner Fn
  and 19w

Howard, Thomas, clk in navy yard; dw n e corner 3e and Ns

Howard, William, carpenter, Ns btw 2 and 3e

Howard, Mrs. widow, 5e near Eastern branch, N Yard

Howard, John, Bn btw 3 and 4e Cap Hill

Howard, Joseph,   ditto

Howard, Henry, shoemaker, s side Fn btw 6 and 7w

Howard, Samuel, blockmaker, Ls btw 8 and 9e N Yard

Howe, Edward, laborer, btw 11 and 12e and L and Ms
  Navy Yard

Howe, Ignatius, 11e near the bridge, Navy Yard

Howle, Lieut. Park G. adjt and inspector marine corps; dw
  14w near Washington bridge

Hughes, Thomas, grocer, s side Pen av near centre market

Hughes, N. coachmaker, 13w btw C and Dn

Hughes, Mary, milliner, s side Fn btw 11 and 12w

Huissy, Philip, fencing master, w side 10w btw E and Fn

Hulbert, Catharine, widow, near corner 7e and Ks N Yard

Humes, John, carpenter, e side 6w btw E and Fn

Humphreys, Charlotte, (col. woman) s side Pen av btw 21
  and 22w

Humphreys, Dolly, (col. woman) Ks btw 8 and 9e N Yard

Hunt, William, bookbinder, s side Dn btw 6 and 7w; dw
  Lou av btw 6 and 7w

Huntt, Henry, M. D. e side 14w btw Pen av and Fn

Hunt, Charles, boot, shoe, and hat store, n side Pen av btw
  9 and 10w

Hunt, Benjamin, bootmaker, 15w near Pen av
Hunter, Thos. painter and glazier, n e corner 20w & Pen av
Hurdle, Thomas, carpenter, 2e near St. Joseph's church
Hurst, Thomas, seaman, opposite N Yard market
Hurley, John Fendall, sparmaker, Ls btw 6 and 7e N Yard
Hutchinson, Edward, 11e near the bridge, N Yard
Hutton, William, carpenter, n side Fn btw 12 and 13w
Hutton, Isaac J. bookbinder, s side Fn btw 13 and 14w
Hutton, James, clk navy coms.' office; dw I n btw 17 & 18w
Hutchinson, John, s side N York av btw 18 and 19w
Hutchinson, Mrs. Samuel, grocery, corner I n and 20w
Hyatt, Seth, grocer, Pen av opposite Indian Queen hotel
Hyatt, Alpheus, grocer, Pen av opposite National hotel

I.

IARDELLA, FRANCIS, carver at the Capitol; dw s side
Pen av btw 1 and 2e Cap Hill
Inch, Philip, painter, 8e near Navy Yard
Ingle, Lindsley and Ingle, hardware merchants, Pen av op-
posite Indian Queen hotel
Ingle, John, (firm of Ingle, Lindsley and Ingle) dw e side
N Jer av btw B and Cs Cap Hill
Ingle, Edward, (firm of Ingle, Lindsley and Ingle) dw Bn
near Pen av
Ingle, Joseph, collector 3d and 4th wards; dw at Eleazer
Lindsley's, s side Pen av btw 4½ and 6w
Ingram, John, (col man) taylor, 7w next to corner Fn
Ironside, Mary, widow, s side Gn btw 13 and 14w
Isherwood, Robert, stonecutter, Gn btw 2 and 3w

J.

JACKSON, ANDREW M'D. clk gen post office; dw at
Mrs Tucker's, s side Pen av near 10w
Jackson, Jacob, (col. man) s e corner 7w and Hn
5

Jackson, Margaret, (col.) washerwoman, 12w near Tiber
   Creek

Jacobs, George, grocer, 7w btw Lou and Dn; dw 11w btw
   Cn and Pen av

James, Elizabeth, widow, e side 14w btw F and Gn

James, William, clk in register's office; dw ditto

Janney, Jacob, shoemaker, Fn btw 12 and 13w

Jarboe, William, s side Ls btw 5 and 6e N Yard

Jarboe, Matthew, keeper Eastern branch middle bridge

Jarvis, Thomas, shipcarpenter, 7e btw L and Ms N Yard

Jeffers, Matthias, plasterer, 13½w btw Pen av and Dn

Jenkins, Hiram, carpenter, Cn near Tiber creek

Jenkins, John, grocer, Pen av near Eastern branch upper
   bridge

Jenifer, Walter H. clk gen land office; Fn btw 19 and 20w

Jesup, Gen. T. S. qr master general; dw Ln btw 16 and 17w

Jett, Thornton, laborer, 11e btw L and Ms N Yard

Jewett, Nathaniel, apothecary, op Mansion hotel, Pen av

Johnson, Richmond, clk surgeon general's office; dw Gn
   west of war office

Johnson, George, clk 1st comptroller's office; dw Georgetown

Johnson, Lewis, tobacco and fancy store, n side Pen av btw
   11 and 12w

Johnson, John, carpenter, s side A s. btw 1 and 2e Cap Hill

Johnson, Martin, printer, n side En btw 9 and 10w

Johnson, Elizabeth, widow, gardener, Mn near Georgetown
   upper bridge

Johnson, Josias S. senator U. States from the state of Louisiana; dw Fn btw 13 and 14w

Johnson, Joseph, captain of the steam boat Independence;
   dw ½w near Eastern branch

Johnson, Thomas, (col. man) sexton Methodist church, Gn
   btw 14 and 15w

Johnson, Spencer, (col. man) shoemaker, s side Pen av btw 21 and 22w

Jolly, Elizabeth, widow, grocery, 7e near navy yard

Jones, Walter, attorney at law, s w corner 12w and Dn

Jones, Raphael, dry goods' store, n e corner Lou av and 3w; dw s w corner 9w and Dn

Jones, col Roger, adjt general; dw n side En btw 8 and 9w

Jones, Edward, ch clk in secretary treasury's office; dw Gay street, Georgetown

Jones, Mr. 10e near Ms N Yard

Jones, William, laborer, I s. near N Jer av

Jones, Joseph, 20 buildings, South Capitol street

Jones, Benjamin, laborer, 11e btw L and Ms N Yard

Jones, William, M. D 13w near Pen av

Jones, Sarah, 12w btw C and Dn

Jones, James, n side Pen av near 23w

Jones, William, (col. man) waiter, Gn btw 13 and 14w

Jones, David, (col. man) shoemaker, e side 13w btw E & Fn

Joyce, Richard, stonecutter, n side Pen av btw 1 and 2w

Joy, Mary, widow, sempstress, w side 9w btw D and En

Judge, John, wheelwright, 11e near bridge, N Yard

Jullien, Honore, confectioner, n side Fn btw 13 and 14w

K.

KAIN, CHARLOTTE, widow, s w corner 4e and Ls

Kean, Stephen R. clothing store, Pen av opposite Indian Queen hotel

Kean, James, grocer, s side East Capitol st opposite the market, Capitol Hill

Keadle, Ann, widow, n e corner Ds and 6e

Kearney, Dr. John A. surgeon U States' navy; dw s w corner Fn and 14w

Kealey, Mary, grocery, corner Vir av and 8e N Yard

Kedzlie, Ann, widow, grocery, n side I n. btw 19 and 20w

Keen, Nathaniel B. currier, Pen av opposite Indian Queen hotel

Keilly, Rev. Jeremiah, principal of the "Washington City College," Capitol Hill

Keller, Jonas, machinist at the patent office; dw corner of Fn and 15w

Keller, J. P. confectioner, dw   ditto

Keller, Frederick, clk in gen land office; dw corner Md av and 12w

Keller, Charles, laborer, 7c btw L and Ms N Yard

Kelly, Lieut. John, at navy yard; dw in the yard

Kellie, Thomas, shipcarpenter, 10c near Ls N Yard

Kelly, James, carpenter, s side Fn opp Catholic church

Kelly, Eliza, grocery, Gn btw 18 and 19w

Kennedy, James, proprietor of the Franklin Inn, n e corner 8w and Dn

Kennedy, John, office of the colonization society, s side Pen av btw 14 and 15w

Kennedy, Andrew T. bookseller and stationer, n side Pen av btw 12 and 13w

Kennedy, John, carpenter, N York av btw 14 and 15w

Kennedy, F. X. coal merchant, n side Pen av btw 9 and 10w

Kennedy, James A. letter carrier, Gn btw 11 and 12w

Kennedy, Mrs. C. E. Hn btw 21 and 22w

Kennedy, L. I. (col. man) barber, 11w btw E and Fu

Kennon, John, carpenter, near the glass house

Kerr, Alexander, cashier Bank of Metropolis, corner Fn and 15w

Kerr, jr. William, printer, w side 6w btw E and Fn

Kervand, L. confectioner, n side Pen av btw 19 and 20w

Keyworth, Robert, watchmaker and jeweller, n side Pen av btw 9 and 10w

Kidwell, George, laborer, 2c btw B and Cn Cap Hill

Kinchy, Paul, confectioner, s side Pen av btw 10 and 11w

King, James, shoemaker, e side 8c btw M and Ns

King, George, wood merchant, 7th st wharf; dw w side 9w btw E and Fn

King, Charles B. portrait painter, 12w btw E and Fn

King, Josias W. clk secretary state's office; dw 17w near war office

King, Robert, draughtsman gen land office; dw 19w btw F and Gn

King, Samuel D. clk in gen land office; dw west of the war office

King, James D clk in 5th auditor's office; dw Georgetown

King, Benjamin, master smith at navy yard; dw 14c near the Eastern branch middle bridge

King, Mary, boarding house, Gn btw 17 and 18w

King, Martin, printer, w side 9w btw D and En

King, Bridget, widow, s side Fn btw 8 and 9w

King, William, bookbinder, ditto

King, Nappy, widow, ditto

King, Mrs. E. widow, e side 14w btw Pen av and Fn

King, Ralph, (col. man) oyster house, s side Cn btw 6 & 7w

Kinsla, Eliza, widow, e side N Jer av btw B & Cs Cap Hill

Kinsley, Benjamin, s side Ks near navy yard market

Kirk, Andrew M. clk 2d auditor's office; dw Georgetown

Kleiber, Jacob, brickmaker, n e corner 3w and Fn

Kleiber, George, carpenter, Lou av btw 6 and 7w

Knapp, Samuel L. attorney at law, w side 7w btw D and En; dw 11w btw F and Gn

Koones, David, clk gen post office; dw Gn btw 11 and 12w

Koontz, Edward, tinner, s side Fn opp Catholic church

Krafft, John M. (city bake house) n e corner Fn and 12w

Kreimer, John, carpenter, n side Dn btw 12 and 13w

Kuhn, Capt. John L. paymaster marine corps; dw Kn btw 23 and 24w

Kurtz, Daniel, clk in Indian department; dw Georgetown

Kustz, Peter, carpenter, w side 8w btw G and Ha

5*

L.

LAMBERT, WILLIAM, mathematician; dw at the Farmers' hotel, Cn west of centre market

Lamble, William, shipcarpenter, Es btw 11 and 12w

Langley, Hezekiah, lumber merchant, s side 12th st wharf, dw near corner Cn and 12w

Langton, William, tinman, s side Pen av btw 17 and 18w

Lanphier, Mrs. Eliza, boarding house, s side Pen av btw 9 and 10w

Lanphier, Robert, engraver and jeweller, at Masi's; dw s side Pen av opposite

Lanham, John, shoemaker, Vir av btw 7 and 8e N Yard

Larned, James, clk 1st comptroller's office; dw 14w btw F and Gn

Larned, James, clk gen land office; dw over Mrs. Dodd's millinery store, Pen av near 15w

Larner, Martin, clk; dw s side En btw 12 and 13w

Larner, Thomas, printer, Dn btw Franklin Inn and office of the National Intelligencer

Larner, Michael, paper carrier, w side 9w btw D and En

Larkum, John, carpenter, s side Dn btw 6 and 7w

Laskey, Richard, tavernkeeper, 7w opp centre market

Latruite, John, watchmaker and jeweller, n side Pen av btw 9 and 10w

Latimer, Marcus, clk 3d auditor's office; dw Georgetown

Laurie, Rev. James, pastor Presbyterian church, Fn, clk in register's office; dw Pen av opposite Mansion hotel

Laub, Andrew M. clk secretary treasury's office; dw Gay st near Rock creek, Georgetown

Laub, John, ch clk first comptroller's office; dw Georgetown

Law, Thomas, N Jer av btw B and Cs

Lawrence, James, tobacconist, n side Pen av btw 3 and 4½w

Lear, B. L. attorney at law, s side Pen av btw 21 and 22w

Leatch, John, cooper, Gn btw 2 and 3w

Lea, George, ornamental painter, 11w near Fn

Leckie, Robert, superintendent of the penitentiary; dw btw 21 and 22w near the glass house

Lee, William, 2d auditor; dw Pen av near Georgetown

Lee, Samuel, blacksmith, 26w near Georgetown up bridge

Lee, John, gardener, Pen av near 6e

Lee, Lewis, (col. man) waiter, Md av near Capitol

Legg, Eli, Farmers' hotel, Ca west of centre market

Legree, John, carpenter, Ls btw 4 and 5e

Lemoon, Joseph, baker, w side N Jer av btw L and Ms

Lenthall, Mrs. widow, 19w btw F and Gn

Lenox, Peter, s side Md av near Washington bridge

Leonard, Jacob, watchmaker at Masi's; dw at Mrs. Franzoni's, opposite new masonic hall

Lepreux, Jane, widow, grocery and confectionary, s w corner Pen av and 12w

Lerras, Susanna, widow, 7e near navy yard

Letourno, Joseph, restaurateur, s side Pen av btw 4½ and 6w

Levering, Thomas, grocery and feed store, e side 7w btw D and En

Lewis, Washington, white and gun smith, n w corner 8w and Dn; dw 5w btw E and Fn

Lewis, Samuel, carpenter, n side En btw 11 and 12w

Lewis, Samuel, clk 2d auditor's office; dw 17w near Van Ness' wharf

Lewis, Edward S. clk 3d auditor's office; dw Greenleaf's Point

Lewis, Frederick, ass't messenger navy department; dw Fn

Lewis, James, (col. man) hostler, 20w near L n near 20w

Lexmouth, Elizabeth, milliner, n e corner Ls & 7e N Yard

Lexmouth, William,   ditto

Leyland, Stephen, bricklayer, 10w btw H and In

Lincoln, William, carpenter, corner Mn and 18w

Lindsay, Adam, councilman 6th ward; dw n e corner Vir av and 7e N Yard

Lindsley, Eleazer, (firm of Ingle, Lindsley and Ingle) dw s side Pen av btw 4½ and 6w

Lipscomb, William C. clk gen post office; dw Georgetown

Lisbee, Thomas, laborer. 10e near Eastern branel

Lisbee, Samuel, laborer, 11e btw I and Ks N Yard

Little, Charles, apothecary and drug store, n side Pen. av btw 19 and 20w

Little, John, Ls btw 6 and 7e N Yard

Little, Peter, clk Navy Yard market, 7e btw H and I s. Navy Yard

Lloyd, William, carpenter, Es btw 10 and 11w

Lloyd, T. tavernkeeper, corner Lou av and Cn

Lloyd, Adam, tinman, Ls btw 8 and 9e N Yard

Lloyd, George, constable, n e corner 1e and Bs Cap Hill

Locke, John B constable, 2e near Md av Cap Hill

Lockwood, John, 1w near old tanyard

Logan, Edward, laborer. 7e near navy yard

Long, James, laborer, Georgia av btw 9 and 10e N Yard

Lonall, Jacob, joiner, Ls btw 8 and 9e N Yard

Lovell, Joseph, surgeon general; dw Pen av opp war office

Lovejoy, John N. messenger 1st comptroller's office; dw Fn btw 1s and 19w

Lowe, Randolph, carpenter, s w corner 6e and Gs N Yard

Lowe, Barbara, corner 3e and Ls

Lowry, William, keeper toll gate at Washington bridge

Lowrie, Allen, engineer steam beat Mount Vernon, 15½w near Md avenue

Lowndes, Francis, clk register's office; dw Georgetown

Lowrie, James H. grocer, s e corner 7w and Fn

Lowrie, Mary, widow, s side Pen av btw 21 and 22w

Lucas, Rev. James, pastor of St. Peter's church, corner Ds and 2e near the church

Lucas, Joshua, carpenter, w side 9w btw D and En
Luxen, William, laborer, n side Pen av btw 22 and 23w
Luxen, Horatio, butcher, w side 7w btw G and Hn
Lutz, John, saddler, s side Pen av btw 17 and 18w
Lydock, Francis, grocer, e side 11w btw E and Fn
Lynch, Ambrose, grocery, n e corner En and 6w
Lyndall, Thomas, master joiner at navy yard; dw I s. btw
 4 and 5e
Lyons, Charles, carpenter, 10w near Cn
Lyons, Mrs. widow, Fn btw 12 and 13w

M.

MACCARDO, M. secretary to Mexican legation, n side
 Fn btw 12 and 13w, at Mrs. Lyons'
Maccubbin, John S. tavernkeeper, n side Cn btw 4½ and 6w
 rear National hotel
Maccubbin, Edward, barber at Brown's hotel
Mackey, William, blacksmith, s e cor 11e and I s. N Yard
Macgill, Thomas, grocer, e side 7w btw F and Gn
Mackey, William, clk register's office; dw Georgetown
Mackey, James, filer, near Fs and 6e N Yard
Machen, Lewis H. clk secretary senate's office; dw Md av
 btw 10 and 11w
Macomb, Gen. Alexander, chief engineer; dw Georgetown
Macdaniel, Ezekiel, clk 4th auditor's office; dw near Rock
 Creek church
Macdaniel, George, clk 4th auditor's office; dw near Rock
 Creek church
Macdaniel, John, clk 4th auditor's office; dw Georgetown
Mackall, L. clk 2d auditor's office; dw Georgetown
Maddox, William R. n e corner Ns and 3e
Magill, Robert, clk 4th auditor's office ; dw Georgetown
Magner, Thomas, tinman, Louisiana av btw 6 and 7w

Maguire, Hugh, teacher, Hn near Penn av

Magruder, Miss Ellen, 2d e btw B and Cs Capitol hill

Major, John, carpenter, w side 6w btw D and En

Marceron, John, carpenter, 10e btw F and Gs Navy Yard

Mallory, Robert, clk in pension office ; dw Georgetown

Marks, Andrew, armorer at marine barracks, Navy Yard

Martin, Agnes, widow, boarding house, n side Dn btw 7 & 8w

Martin, James, laborer, A s. btw 3 and 4e Cap Hill

Martin, James, blacksmith, Penn av btw 1 and 2e Cap hill

Martin, John B. clk 4th aud's office ; dw Fn near 6w

Martin, James, blockmaker, Ms btw 9 & 10e N Yard

Martin, Jacob, ladies' shoemaker, 9e btw L and Ms N Yard

Martin, William, whitesmith, n w corner of Ls and 8e Navy
    Yard

Martin, Philip, laborer, A s btw 3 and 4e Cap Hill

Martin, James, w side 7w btw G and Hn

Martin, William, blockmaker, near Eastern branch, N Yard

Martin, James, white and blacksmith, n side Penn av btw 1
    and 2e Capitol hill

Markwood, William, messenger secretary war's office; dw
    "Goshen," near the slashes

Marshall, Josiah, 14e near Eastern branch

Marshall, George, seaman, Ms btw 9 and 10e N Yard

Marshall, Maria, (col. woman) Dn btw 12 and 13w

Marsh, John, stonecutter, e side N Jer av btw B and Cs

Marr, Catharine, widow, Union st Greenleaf's Point

Marsey, Rachel, 1e btw East Cap st and A s. Cap Hill

Marsillet, Vincent, clk at marine garrison, Navy Yard

Marvel, Charles, (col. man) n side Fn btw 12 and 13w

Masters, William, joiner, 7e btw F and Gs N Yard

Massi, F. professor of music, n side Pen av btw 9 and 10w

Massi, Vincent, dancing master, dw   ditto

Massi, Seraphim, jeweller, silversmith, and watchmaker,
    n side Pen av btw 4½ and 6w

Mason, William, saddler, n side Pen av btw 4½ and 6w

Matthews, Rev. William, pastor of St. Patrick's church; n e corner Fn and 10w

Matthews, Henry C. clk 3d auditor's office ; dw Georgetown

Mattingly, Edward, grocer and tavernkeeper 3e near the Eastern branch

Matlock. Simeon, merchant tailor, e side New Jer av btw B and Cs Capitol hill

Matlock, Jeremiah, tailor, 8w btw G and Hn

Maury, Richard B., Register, Navy dept ; dw Georgetown

Maul, John P s side Penn av btw 19 and 20w

Mauro, Philip (firm of Mauro and Son) n w corner Penn av and 7w ; dw w side 6w near Unitarian church

Mauro, William, (firm of Mauro and Son) ; ditto   [hill

May, Frederick, M. D. e side New Jer av btw B and Cs Cap

May, George W., M. D. n e corner of 9w and Dn

M'Carty, Mrs. widow, 10w btw D and En

M'Carty, John, mess. war dept s side Penn av btw 18 & 19w

M'Carty, Mr. tailor, n side Penn av btw 4½ and 3n

M'Carty, Florence, shoemaker, s side Fn btw 6 and 7w

M'Causland, Margery, boarding house, Pen av btw 17 & 18w

M'Cauley, Mrs. Elizabeth, widow, s side Pen av btw 10 & 11w

M'Cauley, William M coppersmith, and sealer of weights and measures, s side Penn av btw 12 and 13w

M'Cerren, Andrew, carpenter, s e corner of Dn and 13w

M'Clery, James, clk Register's office ; dw Fn btw 14 and 15w

M'Clelland, John, brickmaker, New York av opposite 2d Presbyterian church

M'Closker, Hugh, grocer, e side 7w btw Lou av and Dn

M'Clannan, William, bricklayer, 7e near Navy Yard

M'Cormick, Rev. Andrew T. clk secretary of state's office ; dw Bs btw 1e and New Jer av Capitol hill

M'Cormick, William J. common councilman, and post master House of Representatives, s side East Capitol st btw 1 and 2 e Capitol hill

M'Cormick, Thomas, grocer, ditto

M'Corkle, Joseph P. clk navy commissioners' office ; dw at
   Mr. Nourse's, Washington heights
M'Conchy, Richard, cabinet maker, En btw 9 and 10w
M'Conchy, Walter, ditto
M'Coy, Robert, carpenter, A s. btw 1 and 2e Capitol Hill
M'Coy, George, (col. man) plasterer, En btw 14 and 15w
M'Culloch, Robert, carpenter, btw 9 and 10w and E and Fn
M'Cutchen, John, grocer, Lou av btw 6 and 7w
M'Daniel, Elizabeth, widow, e side 11w near Pen av
M'Daniel, William, laborer, Ls. btw 3 and 4e
M'Dermott, Michael, hackman, Lou av btw 6 and 7w
M'Donald, John G. ch clk secretary of Senate's office: dw
   Md avenue, near Capitol square
M'Donald, William, grocer, corner 13½ and Es
M'Donald, Alexander, messenger register's office; dw near
   U. S. Branch bank
M'Donald, John, (col. man) barber, 6w opp National hotel
M'Dowell, William, shipcarpenter, Ls btw 8 and 9e N Yard
M'Dowell, Sarah, spinster, 14w near the Tiber
M'Duell, John, painter, n.e corner Pen av and 11w
M'Duell, George, dealer, s side Fn btw 12 and 13w
M'Elwee, Samuel, printer, n e corner 6w and En
M'Farland, John, joiner, 7e btw F and Gs N Yard
M'Farlane, George, bricklayer, 10e btw I and Ks N Yard
M'Gilpin, William, caulker, 11e near bridge, N Yard
M'Gill, Mr. keeper of toll gate at Navy Yard bridge
M'Gilton, William B. caulker, 11e near Bs
M'Gowan, Ann, widow, w side 11w btw E and Fn
M'Gowan, Patrick, Gn near 7w
M'Gunnigle, Ann, widow, 10w btw Pen av and Fn
M'Henry, Jonathan, shipwright, Ms btw 9 and 10e N Yard
M'Intosh, Thomas, stonecutter, Bn btw 1 and 2e Cap Hill
M'Intire, Ruth, widow, boarding house, Pen av btw 4½ & 6w
M'Intire, Alexander, clk patent office; dw near 17w & I n

M'Kean, Saml. clk war department; dw near Quaker meeting house

M'Kenny, Thomas L. Indian department; dw Georgetown

M'Kenny, Benson, carpenter, 11e near bridge, N Yard

M'Lean, John, postmaster general; dw n side Cn btw 4½ & 6w

M'Lean, Cornelius, carpenter, Pen av btw 13 and 14w

M'Leod, John, teacher Washington Central Academy, n side Fn btw 13 and 14w

M'Minn, Mary Ann, e side 10w btw E and Fn

M'Leod, John, clk in gen post office; dw w side N Jer av btw B and Cs Cap Hill

M'Nechany, Edward, Union st Greenleaf's Point

M'Quillan, John, stonecutter, A s. btw 1 and 2e Cap Hill

M'Ren, A. carpenter, corner Da and 13w

M'Williams, Alexander A., M. D. I s. btw 6 and 7e N Yard

M'Williams, Clement, wood merchant, n w corner 13½w near Washington bridge

Meade, Richard W. Pen av near 6 buildings

Mechlin, William, clk 2d auditor's office; dw I n. btw 17 and 18w

Mechlin, Joseph, clk 4th auditor's office; dw 20w opposite western market

Medley, Thomas, saddler, 16w btw I an I K n

Meehan, John, printer, U. States' Telegraph, e side 10w btw D and En

Metlin, James, bricklayer, near the glass house

Metzgr, William, tanner, 2e near N Jer avenue

Middleton, James, carpenter, Union st Greenleaf's Point

Middleton, Erasmus J. secretary board of aldermen; dw 6e btw D and Es

Milburn, Draden, widow, 5e btw K and Ls N Yard

Milburn, Mr. tavernkeeper, s side Fn near 13w

Miles, James, commission merchant, s side Pen av btw 10 and 11w

Miles, Edward, carpenter, Gn btw 2 and 3e

Miller, Thomas, clk navy dep't; dw 6 buildings, Pen av

Miller, Hezekiah, clk Indian department, dw Georgetown

Miller, Henry, brickmaker, w side 13w btw F and Gn

Miller, Lawrence, shoemaker, n e corner 10e and Ms Navy Yard

Miller, Charles, butcher, 9e opposite N Yard

Millard, Joshua, corner Bs and 13½w

Miles, Mrs. widow, corner N Jer av and Ks

Milstead, Barton, brickmaker, w side N Jer av btw L & Ms

Milstead, Ignatius, tavernkeeper, n w corner Md av and 13½w near Washington bridge

Milstead, Judson, brickmaker, 1w btw M and Ns

Milstead, Peter, w side N Jer av btw L and Ms

Minchen, Patience, widow, N Jer av btw B and Cs Cap Hill

Mitchell, Thomas S. carpenter, e side 8w btw G and Hn

Mitchell, Richard, keeper of bridge tavern, Navy Yard

Mockbee, Ellen, 13 w near Tiber Creek

Mohun, Philip, laborer, 3w btw F and Gn

Monan, Harrison, laborer, Geo av btw 11 and 12e N Yard

Moody, J. shoemaker, corner Pen av and 10e

Moore, Valinda, widow, w side 10w btw D and En

Moore, John M. ch clk gen land office; dw 1 n. btw 17 & 18w

Moore, James, messenger and asst. clk treasurer's office; dw 10w btw D and En

Moore, Thomas, carpenter, Ln btw 19 and 20w

Moore, jr. James, butcher, Cn rear of Farmers' hotel, near centre market

Moore, John, butcher, corner 4½ and Is Greenleaf's Point

Moore, Nathan, constable, s side Pen av opp western mk't

Moore, Alexander C. hairdresser, n side Lou av near 9w

Morgan, Ann, widow, 1s near N Jer av

Morgan, Ann, widow, boarding house, 13w opposite Washington Assembly Rooms

Moreland, H. B. boarding house, over Allens' lottery office, n side Pen av btw 6 and 7w

Morfit, Henry M. attorney at law, n e corner Pen and 4½w
Morris, Anthony, clk register's office; dw 7 buildings
Mortison, William M. furniture warehouse, s side Pen av
btw 3 and 4½w
Moran, Sarah, widow, near corner En and 11w
Morris, Peggy, Ms btw 4½ and Union st Greenleaf's Point
Morton, William, clk 1st auditor's office; dw n e corner of
Washington and West sts Georgetown
Morton, Mr Ns btw 4½ and Union sts Greenleaf's Point
Moss, P. tavernkeeper, n side Ls btw 7 and 8e N Yard
Moulder, John N. clk in 2d comptroller's office, dw I n btw
21 and 22w
Mountz, Joseph, clk register's office; dw Gn btw 17 & 18w
Mudd, Thos. J. carpenter, Mn near Georgetown up bridge
Mudd, Ignatius, inspector of lumber, s c corner Ds & 13½w
Mudd, Walter, s side Kn near Georgetown lower bridge
Mudd, Edward, laborer, w side 7e btw K and Ls N Yard
Mulliken, Thomas, e side 6w btw E and Fn
Mulliken, N. shoemaker, n side Pen av btw 9 and 10w
Munroe, Thomas, city postmaster; dw 7 buildings
Munroe, Columbus, clk city post office; dw ditto
Munroe, David, carpenter, w side 12w btw E and Fn
Murphy, J. D. blacksmith, 13w btw Pen av and Dn
Murphy, Esther, widow, 9e near marine barracks, N Yard
Murray, Michael, n side Pen av btw 3 and 4½w
Murray, Thomas, grocery, 7w opposite centre market
Muse, Lindsay, waiter, 26w btw I and Kn
Muse, Charlotte, (col.) washerwoman; Pen av btw 19 & 20w
Mustin, Thomas, ch clerk 5th auditor's office; dw corner
Fn and 20w
Myer, Franklin S. printing office, corner Pen av and 10w
Myer, Salome, widow, boarding house, 7w opp centre m'kt
Myers, Benjamin B. grocer, s side Pen av btw 11 and 12w
Myers, John B. saddler, n side Pen av btw 4½ and 6w
Myerson, James, shipcarpenter, 7e btw K and Ls N Yard

N.

NAILER, MARTHA, widow, tailoress, s side Pen av btw
3 and 4½w

Nairn, James, carver and stonecutter, corner 13½w and Cr

Nally, Letitia, spinster, 3e btw I and Ks

Nardin, Mary, tavern and cook shop, Lou av btw 6 and 7w

Nash, Patrick F. shoemaker, 7e btw L and Ms N Yard

Neale, Henry C. register of wills, w side 13w btw E and Fi

Nesmith, Ann, widow, 7e near navy yard

Nevitt, Ann, widow, 5e near Eastern branch

Nevins, John S. clk 5th auditor's office; dw Georgetown

Newell, Robert, clk secretary treasury's office; lln btw 15
and 16w

Newell, Jonas, shoemaker, n side Pen av btw 10 and 11w

Nicholson, Peter, caulker, near corner 5e and Es

Nicholson, Charity, widow, 8e btw Vir av and I s. N Yard

Noerr, Andrew, German bakehouse, s side Fn btw 13 & 14w

Nokes, James, painter, n w corner Ks and 10e Navy Yard

Nolen, John, sparmaker, near Eastern branch, N Yard

Nolen, James, tailor, next to corner 19w and Pen av

Norman, Jane, widow, 3e btw East Cap st and A s. Cap Hill

Nottall, Benjamin, n side Pen av btw 1 and 2e Cap Hill

Nott, James, messenger, s side Bs btw 1e and N Jer av
Capitol Hill

Nott, Lewis, 3e btw East Cap st and A s. Cap Hill

Nottingham, Mary, widow, 13w btw C and Dn

Nourse, Joseph, register of the treasury; dw heights above
Georgetown

Nourse, Col. Michael, ch clk in register's office; dw 13w
btw E and Fn

Nourse, C. J. chief clk in secretary of war's office; dw 7
buildings, Pen av

Nourse, John, clk in register's office; dw heights above
Georgetown

Nowland, John, model maker at navy yard; dw 11c opp navy yard

Nowland, E. S. 13w btw C and Dn

Noyes, Catharine, widow, w side 7w btw G and Hn

Noyes, Thomas L. clk in city post office; dw ditto

O.

OBREGON, DON PABLO, minister plenipotentiary from the republic of Mexico; s side Fn opposite the bank of Metropolis

O'Brien, Michael, laborer, 13½w btw C and D₃

O'Bryon, James, printer, e side 8w btw D and En

O'Donnell, Barny, steward at navy hospital, n w corner Pen av and 10c [Point

O'Donnell, Hugh, brewer, btw 4½ and Union st Greenleaf's

O'Halloran, William, stonecutter, w side 8w btw G and Hn

Olive, Ann, (firm of Olive and Beatty) milliner and mantua maker, corner 14w and Pen av

O'Neale, William, I n opposite western market

O'Neale, Mrs. John, gardener, 20w near western grave yard

O'Neale, John, weaver, w side 9w btw D and En

O'Neale, James, laborer, near Eastern branch and ½ st w

Ord, James, magistrate, Gn btw 18 and 19w

Ormes, Mary, widow, s side Fn btw 7 and 8w

Orme, Resin, lumber merchant; n side 12th st wharf; dw s side Fn btw 10 and 11w

Orr, John, gardener, n w corner Fn and 8w

Orr, Henry, (col. man) laborer, 19w btw F and Gn

Orr, Obed, carpenter, 10 buildings

Osbourn and Barnes, dry goods' store, s side Pen av btw 6 and 7w

Osborn, James, bricklayer, 8w btw G and Hn

Osborn, Dennis, blacksmith at navy yard; dw C₃ near Eastern branch

Osgardby, Thomas, laborer, Mn btw 17 and 18w

Otis, William, clk gen land office; dw at Mrs. M'Cardle's, Capitol Hill

Otterbach, Philip, butcher, corner Ms and 9e N Yard

Ould, Henry, teacher western public school, s e corner Gn and 14w; dw corner 12w and Gn

Our, David, grocer, s side East Cap st opposite market, Capitol Hill

Ourand, Elijah, sweepmaster, 18w btw H and I n

Overton, Isaac, Hn btw 6 and 7w

Owen, Mary, Hn btw 18 and 19w

Owner, James, master shipwright at navy yard; dw n side Ks btw 9 and 10e N Yard

Owner, William, dry goods' store, n side Lou av btw 8 & 9w

Overstreet, Amos, teacher, s w corner Ks and 10e N Yard

P.

PACKARD, PEREZ, dairyman, Hn btw 5 and 6w

Padgett, Joseph, shipcarpenter, Ls btw 8 and 9e N Yard

Page, Daniel, joiner, I s. btw 6 and 7e N Yard

Painter, John, laborer, Gn near 7w

Pairo, Thomas W. dry goods' store, n side Pen av next to corner 11w

Palmer, Susan, w side 11w near corner Hn

Palmer, Pennell, hat store, n side Pen av btw 6 and 7w

Pancoast, David, carpenter, 2e btw A s. and East Capitol street, Capitol Hill

Parker, Gen. Daniel, corner 21w and Hn

Panham, Benjamin, shoemaker, n side Dn btw 6 and 7w

Parker, William, ch clk 1st auditor's office; dw 6 buildings, Pen avenue

Parker and Co. grocers, Lou av btw 7 and 8w opp centre market

Parker, George, coachmaker, Hn btw 17 and 18w

Parker, Simeon, carpenter, Gn btw 18 and 19w

Parker, Charles, (col. man) 14w near Pen av

Parsons, Thomas, boarding house, e side 9w btw D and En

Parsons, William, blacksmith, near Eastern branch, N Yard

Parsons, Joseph, 11c near the bridge, Navy Yard

Parsons, Burnet, carpenter, n w corner Bs and 4e

Passett, Peter, upholsterer, s e corner Pen av and 11w

Patterson, Charles W. baker, n side I n. btw 19 and 20w

Patterson, Robert, (col. man) blacksmith, Missouri av near the canal

Payne, John, carpenter, near Georgetown lower bridge

Payne, John, (col. man) carpenter, 15w near Ln

Peake, John, pilot, Ls btw 4 and 5e Navy Yard

Peake, Thomas, laborer, dw   ditto

Pearl, Ann, sempstress, 13w btw Pen av and Dn

Pearcey, William, lieutenant U. S. Navy, Navy Yard

Pease, Frances, widow, w side 8w btw E and Fn

Pease, Alfred, s side Md av near Washington bridge

Peck, Hiel, boarding house, corner Pen av and 15w

Pelton, Eliza, widow, Hn btw 18 and 19w

Penn, William, brickmaker, I s. near N Jer avenue

Penn, Edward, blacksmith, near En and 11w

Perkins, Jeremiah, painter, s side Ks near N Yard market

Perrin, Noel, gardener, n e corner Md av and 7w

Peters, John, clk 2d auditor's office; dw heights of Georgetown

Pettit, John, dyer and scourer, Cn btw 4½ and 6w

Petit, Charles, carpenter, En btw 5 and 6w

Petit, Augustus, carpenter, s side Pen av btw 12 and 13w

Petitjean, Auguste, distiller of cordials, 11w near Pen av

Peters, William, shipcarpenter, 4e btwK and Ls N Yard

Peters, John, (col. woman) corner of 15w and Mn

Peyton, Ann Eliza, 4½w btw Pen av and Cn

Phillips, George, stonecutter, n side East Cap st near market, Capitol Hill

Phillips, Jonathan, printer, 7w btw F and Gn (back)

Phillips, Stephen, carpenter, n e corner 7w and Fn

Pic, John, keeper of the Phœnix porter cellar, Vir avenue near 8e Navy Yard

Pickett, Mason, hatter, Lou av btw 6 and 7w

Pierce, Daniel, umbrella maker, n side Pen av btw 3 & 4½w

Pitts, William, printer, e side 7w near Fn

Plant, James, cabinet maker, s w corner Pen av and 10w

Pleasanton, Stephen, 5th auditor; dw corner Fn and 20w

Plumley, Alexander R. teacher, Hn btw 17 and 18w

Poleta, Joseph, runner at war office; dw w side 10w btw E and Fn

Polk, Miss Ann, boarding house, Pen av op Mansion hotel

Polk, David P. printer; dw at Mrs. Lanphier's, Pen avenue

Polkinhorn, Charles, saddler, n side Pen av btw 4½ and 6w

Polkinhorn, Richard W. dw   ditto

Poor, Moses, auctioneer and com. merchant, and agent for the Ætna Insurance Company, s side Pen av btw 4½ and 6w; dw w side 7w btw E and Fn

Poor, Nathaniel P. auctioneer and commission merchant, s side Pen av btw 4½ and 6w

Pope, Eleanor, widow, sempstress, Fs btw 7 and 8e N Yard

Pope, Frederick, blacksmith, Vir av btw 7 and 8e N Yard

Porter, Daniel P. clk 1st auditor's office; dw Pen av btw 21 and 22w

Post, Rev. Reuben, pastor 1st Presbyterian church; dw S. Capitol street, next door south of church

Poston, Fielder, n side Kn near Georgetown lower bridge

Posey, Kitty, (col. woman) Dn btw 12 and 13w

Posey, Francis, (col. man) laborer, Gn btw 14 and 15w

Pottinger, Thomas, clk 5th auditor's office; dw Georgetown

Potts, John, baker, 11w near Pen avenue

Powell, Elizabeth, widow, s e corner 2e and Ds

Powers, Joseph, carpenter, s side Bs btw N Jer av and 1e Capitol Hill

Prentiss, William, asst. messenger and watchman state department; dw e side 11w btw E and Fn

Preston, Anthony, slater, w side 12w btw G and Hn

Pressey, Mr. joiner, Ms btw 9 and 10e N Yard

Price, Benjamin, 10e near Ms N Yard

Prime, William, painter, 7e btw F and Gn N Yard

Pringle, Elizabeth, 11w near En

Pritchard, Arthur, carpenter, Cn near Washington Assembly Rooms

Prout, Jonathan, dry goods' store, s w corner 8e and Ls Navy Yard

Prout, William, dry goods' store, s side Pen av btw 6 and 7w; dw 7w btw D and En

Proctor, (col. man) laborer, s side the Tiber, opposite centre market

Pryse, Charles, gold and silversmith, s side Pen av btw 12 and 13w

Pullizzi, Felice, musician in marine band; dw 1s near 7e Navy Yard

Pullizzi, Venerando, sergeant of marines; dw in navy yard

Pumphrey, Lloyd, contractor for building stone; 3e btw East Capitol st and A s. Capitol Hill

Pumphrey, Rezin, laborer, btw 11 and 12e and L and Ms Navy Yard

Purdy, John, painter and glazier, n side Pen av west of and near the Capitol

Purnell, Mrs. widow, Ms btw 9 and 10e Navy Yard

Q.

QUEEN, R. T. clk 2d auditor's office; dw Georgetown

Queen, Nicholas L boarding house, 1e btw East Capitol street and A s. fronting Capitol square

Queen, Elizabeth, boarding house, s side Pen av near centre market

Queen, Eliza, boarding house, Bn near Del av Cap Hill

Queen, John, master bricklayer, at the Capitol; dw corner 2e and Bn Capitol Hill

Queen, William, (col. man) s w corner 7w and Hn

R.

RAMSAY, WILLIAM, clk in 3d auditor's office; dw Fn near 20w

Randall, Richard, M. D opposite Mansion hotel, Pen av

Randolph, P. S. clk navy commissioners' office; dw at Mrs. Tucker's, Pen av

Randall, Henry, clk 3d auditor's office; dw 7 buildings

Randolph, William B. clk register's office; dw Alexandria county

Rapine, Mrs. widow, w side N Jer av btw B & Cs Cap Hill

Ratcliffe, Joseph, grocer, next to n w corner 7e and Ls Navy Yard

Rawling, John, dry goods' store, n side Pen av near seven buildings

Read, Robert, clk 3d auditor's office; dw Georgetown

Reed, Josiah F. printer, n side Dn btw 6 and 7w

Reed, Isaac, (col. man) laborer, Ds btw 2 and 3e

Redfin, Samuel, grocer, n e corner Pen av and 19w

Reilly, John, clk bank of Washington; dw w side 12w btw Pen av and En

Reilly, Thomas B. clk 1st comptroller's office; dw Eldon Hill

Reiling, John, butcher, Ms btw 11 and 12e N Yard

Remmley, John, carpenter, Fn. btw 17 and 18w

Reynolds, William, gardener, n side Pen av btw 22 and 23w

Rhea, Daniel, boot and shoemaker, Pen av btw 17 and 18w

Rhodes, Thompson, clk engineer dep't; dw Georgetown

Rhodes, James, bricklayer, 10e near Ms Navy Yard

Rice, Patrick, stonecutter, w side 7w btw Lou av and Dn

Rice, Edward, shoemaker, corner Bs and 1e Capitol Hill

Richardson, Luke, scavenger 3d ward, corner Nn near 14w

Richards, Mrs. widow, 7e btw L and Ms Navy Yard

Riddall, William, clk ordnance department; dw En near 13w

Ridgeley, William G. clk navy commissioners' office; dw Georgetown

Rigsby, Stanislaus, blacksmith, Vir av btw 3 and 4e

Rigden, Thomas, watchmaker, n side Fn btw 13 and 14w

Riggals, Thomas, scavenger 1st ward, n e corner 16w & I n.

Ringgold, Tench, marshal of the District of Columbia; dw n w corner Fn and 18w

Ringgold, Thomas G. clk ordnance dep't; dw Georgetown

Riorden, James, exchange bookstore, n side Pen av btw 4½ and 6w   [of Georgetown

Rittenhouse, B. Franklin, clk register's office; dw heights

Rives, John C. clerk United States' Telegraph; dw Brown's hotel

Rivers, Hanson, blacksmith, Ls btw 8 and 9e N Yard

Roach, John, blacksmith, 6w btw Cs and Louisiana av

Roberdeau, Col. chief topographical engineers; dw Georgetown

Roby, Washington, tavernkeeper, e side 9w btw D and En

Roby, Thomas, laborer, corner Geo av and 11e N Yard

Roby, Ann, widow, 10e opposite Navy Yard

Robinson, Elizabeth, widow, 10 buildings, N Jer avenue

Robinson, Thomas, carpenter, En near Pen avenue

Robinson, Philip, shoemaker,   ditto

Robinson, Mary, s side Pen av btw 9 and 10w

Robinson, Samuel, dry goods' store, s side Pen av btw 4½ and 6w

Rodgers, Com. John, of the U. S. navy; dw Ps btw 4½ and the Potomac, Greenleaf's Point

Rollins, John, carpenter, Dn btw 12 and 13w

Rollins, Joshua, boatman, Dn near Tiber Creek

Rollins, John, painter, 11e btw L and Ms Navy Yard

Ronckendorff, Mary, widow, confectioner, n side Pen av btw 4½ and 6w

Rose, Samuel, confectioner, n side Pen av near Georgetown

Rose, John, machinist at navy yard; dw 8e btw G and Is

Rose, Robert, foreman gun carriage maker at navy yard; dw corner Vir av and 7e Navy Yard

Rose, C widow, 7e btw K and Ls Navy Yard

Ross, M. clk gen post office; dw at Mr. Blair's, 6w near the post office

Ross, Daniel, laborer, Bs btw 1 and 2e Capitol Hill

Roscop, Jacob, butcher, n side East Cap st btw 1 and 2e

Rostridge, James. laborer, Ks btw 8 and 9e Navy Yard

Rothwell, Andrew, printer, e side 11w btw Pen av and En

Rothwell, Miss E. silk button maker; dw   ditto

Rowland and Greer, printers, w side N Jer av 2d house south of the Capitol

Rowan, James, painter, s side Fn btw 13 and 14w

Roxburgh, Absalom, boatman, Fn btw 24 and 25w

Ruddock, Samuel A. clk gen post office; dw at Carothers', s e corner Pen av and 6w

Rumpff, Henry, runner in the Patriotic bank; dw s side Fn btw 10 and 11w

Runnells, Sarah Ann, widow, 10 buildings

Rush, Richard, secretary of the treasury; dw 18w west of the war office

Russ, Francis, sparmaker, e side 7e btw H and I s. N Yard

Rusket, John, hairdresser, Ks btw 8 and 9e N Yard

Russell, Frederick A coachmaker, n side Pen av btw 4½ and 6w; dw n side Pen av btw 1 and 2w

Russell, John, laborer, n side Pen av btw 22 and 23w

Ryan, Henry, carpenter, Hn btw 9 and 10w

Ryland, Rev. William, pastor of Ebenezer church; 8e opp marine barracks

S.

SALOMON, LEWIS, clk in register's office; dw 19w btw I and Kn

Samuels, William, shoemaker, s side Fn btw 6 and 7w

Sanderson, Thomas, plumber, 11e near the bridge, N Yard

Sanderson, William, ditto

Sanders, Sarah, widow, e side 12w near Pen av

Sandford, Thomas, grocer, s side East Capitol st opposite the market, Capitol Hill

Sandy, Henry, carpenter, Dn btw 12 and 13w

Sandiford, jr. Thomas, carpenter, n side Gn btw 20 & 21w

Sandiford, Phœbe, I n btw 20 and 21w

Sanford, George, lumber yard at Coombe's wharf; dw corner 3e and Ls

Sanford, John, constable, Ks btw 8 and 9e N Yard

Sanders, Ann, (col.) washerwoman, 14w near Pen av

Saoussa, John, messenger at the U. S. Branch bank, near corner 12w and N York avenue

Saunders, David, clk gen post office; dw Fn btw 7 and 8w

Savage, George, brushmaker, corner 9w and Pen av; dw 11w near Fn

Savage, John, stage driver, s side Pen av btw 3 and 4½w

Sawyer, William M. n side Lou av btw 6 and 7w

Sawkins, William, watchmaker, n side Pen av btw 12 & 13w

Scallan, James, foreman plumber at navy yard; dw Vir av btw 6 and 7e N Yard

Schaeffter, George F. baker, An btw 1 and 2e Cap Hill

Scholfield, Joseph, w side 8w btw D and En

Schley, Thomas, plasterer, corner Hn and 18w

Schooley, Elizabeth, 26w btw I and Kn

Scott, Thomas C, M. D. s side Pen av btw 6 and 7w

Scott, James S. clk gen post office; dw I n near Friends' meeting house

Scott, A. Pen av btw 19 and 20w

Scott, Thomas, carpenter, 28w near Georgetown Pr bridge

Scott, Horatio, coppersmith, 5e near Eastern branch

Scott, Alexander, w side N Jer av btw B and Cs Cap Hill

Scott, Rebecca, widow, Ks near Eastern branch up. bridge

Scott, John, laborer,   ditto

Scott, George, Ls   ditto

Scott, Theodore, laborer, Ls btw 6 and 7e N Yard

Scott, Richard, (col. man) oyster house, Pen av btw 19 and 20w

Scrivener, Samuel, shoemaker, corner Indiana av and 3w

Seaver, Mrs. now Mrs. M. Bowen, widow, milliner and ladies' dress maker, n side Penn av btw 9 and 10w

Sedwick, Sally, milliner, s side Pen av btw 6 and 7w

Selden, Cary, naval storekeeper, n w corner 3e and Cs Capitol Hill

Selby, Philip, laborer, Gn btw 2 and 3w

Sengstack, C. P. house and sign painter, s side Pen av btw 12 and 13w

Sendorff, Joseph, shoemaker, corner Cn and 12w

Serrin, Daniel, carpenter, 26w near Georgetown up bridge

Serrin, William, constable, Kn btw 21 and 22w

Sessford, John, messenger 2d comptroller's office; dw s side Dn near 12w

Sessford James, tobacconist, n side Pen av btw 3 and 4½w

Sessford and Offutt, painters, e side 10w btw D and En

Sewall, Thomas, M. D. s side Pen av near centre market

Sewall, Maria, (col.) washerwoman, 3w btw F and Gn

Shanks, Michael, china and glass store, n side Pen av btw 9 and 10w

Shaw, Eleanor, widow, sempstress, Fs btw 7 and 8e N Yard

Shaw, Ann, widow, 5e btw East Cap st and A s. Cap Hill

Shay, Elijah, n side Pen av btw 22 and 23w

Shelton, Moses, shipcarpenter, Vir av btw 9 & 10e N Yard

Shedden, Mrs. widow, seminary for young ladies, s side Pen av btw 10 and 11w

Sheckles, John, boarding house, 7w btw F and Gn

Shepherd, Joseph, boatman, 11w near Tiber creek

Shepherd, L. barber, n side Pen av near Mansion hotel

Sherwood, Samuel, printer, w side 11w btw E and Fn

Sherlock, John, bookbinder, s side Fn btw 6 and 7w

Shields, Thomas, hairdresser at the National hotel; dw Lou av near city hall

Shields, Mrs. widow, 5w opposite city hall

Shoemaker, David, clk gen land office; dw upper end of High street, Georgetown

Shorter, Margaret, widow, washerwoman, Pen av near 6e

Sibley, John, blacksmith, near corner 18w and Mn

Silence, John, shoemaker, Dn btw 12 and 13w

Simms, Mrs. widow, Pen av near 6e

Simms, Edward, grocer, 8e btw I and Ks N Yard

Sims, John D. clk navy department; dw Pen av opposite six buildings

Sim, Thomas, M. D. near the western market

Simmons, William, clk gen land office; dw 8w near general post office

Simpson, M. T. agent gen post office; dw at John Davis', Cn btw 4½ and 6w

Simpson, Presley, clk gen post office; dw near western extremity of Pen avenue

Simpson, Ann, Cn near Tiber creek

Simpson, Josiah, 12w near Cn

Simpson, Tobias, (col. man) messenger, A s. btw 2 and 3e

Sinnott, Margaret, schoolmistress, s side Fn btw 6 and 7w

Sinon, John, tailor, Lou av btw 8 and 9w

Sinclair, James, blacksmith, 26w near Georgetown upper bridge

Sinclair, Sarah, schoolmistress, corner 7w and Fn

Skidmore, George, blacksmith, 13½w btw Pen av and Dn

Skinner, I. L. principal of young ladies' academy, n side Fn, next to corner 9w

Slade, William, clk secretary state's office; dw 14w btw
    F and Gn

Slade, Thomas, hackman, w side 6w btw F and Gn

Slight, Pringle, carpenter, near 2w and Vir av

Slye, Thomas G. clk 1st auditor's office; dw Georgetown

Slye, Robert A. clk navy coms' office; dw   ditto

Smallwood, William A. lumber merchant, Vir av btw 3 & 4e

Smallwood, Dorothy, widow, 3e btw M and Ns

Smallwood, John, shipcarpenter, n w corner 10e and Ks
    Navy Yard

Smallwood, Abraham, laborer, 11w btw Md av and Es

Smether, Dr. R. dentist, n side Pen av btw 4½ and 6w

Smith, Samuel H. president bank of Washington; dw in the
    country

Smith, Richard, cashier Branch U. S. bank; dw west of and
    adjoining the bank ·

Smith, Henry, carpenter, e side 11w btw E and Fn

Smith, Nathan, carpenter, e side 7w btw E and Fn

Smith, Fleet, attorney at law, n side Gn btw 11 and 12w; of-
    fice, ditto

Smith, Mrs. A. W. milliner, n side Pen av btw 9 and 10w

Smith, Francis Linnæus, clk secretary of state's office; dw
    seven buildings

Smith, J. D. shoemaker, n side Pen av next to corner 12w

Smith, J. C. R wine and liquor store, Lou av btw 8 and 9w

Smith, John, shipcarpenter, 11e btw L and Ms N Yard

Smith, Robert, 20w btw Pen av and Hn

Smith, William, e side 3e near Eastern branch

Smith, Elizabeth, widow, s w corner 11w and Hn

Smith, Elizabeth, widow, w side N Jer av btw I and Ks

Smith, Cornelius, shipcarpenter, Geo av btw 11 and 12e
    Navy Yard

Smith, Francis, laborer, btw 11 and 12e and L and Ms
    Navy Yard

Smith, James, rigger at navy yard; dw Ls btw 2 and 3e

Smith, John A. clk in clerk's office circuit court; dw 5w btw Lou av and En

Smith, Mrs widow, n e corner 10e and Ms Navy Yard

Smith, Thomas, livery stable, 19w btw Pen av and I n.

Smith, John, sweepmaster 3d and 4th wards; dw n side Pen av btw 3 and 4½w

Smith, Rev. David (col.) pastor of the African church; dw near St. Peter's church, Ds Cap Hill

Smith, John, grave digger, 7e btw F and Gs N Yard

Smith, Thomas, (col. man) hackman, Vir av btw 3 and 4e

Smith, Thomas, (col. man) boatman, near the glass house

Smoot, George A. clk at Langley's lumber yard; dw e side 11w btw E and Fn

Smoot, John H. carpenter, Ls btw 11 and 12e N Yard

Smoot, William, cabinet maker; 7e btw L and Ms N Yard

Smoot, Samuel, n side Kn near Georgetown lower bridge

Somerville, Robert, (col. man) tanner, I s. near N Jer av

Southard, Samuel L. secretary of the navy; dw 16w fronting President's square

Southerland, Thomas I. messenger in 4th auditor's office; dw s side En btw 10 and 11w

Southerland, William, stonecutter, n side Pen av btw 1 and 2e Capitol Hill

Spalding, John, master gunsmith at navy yard; dw n w corner 6e and Es

Spalding, John, 3e btw M and Ns

Spalding, Richard, constable, near navy magazine

Spalding, Francis, bricklayer, w side 12w near Pen av

Spalding, Enoch, grocery, 14w btw C and Dn

Speake, Mary Ann, widow, s e corner Fn and 10w

Speake, John, shoemaker, n side Fn btw 6 and 7w

Speake, John B. s side Fn btw 13 and 14w

Speiden, William, clk at purser's store, navy yard; dw n w corner 4e and Vir avenue

Speiden, Robert, 4e btw Gs and Vir avenue

7*

Speiden, John, ship carpenter, 7e btw K and Ls N Yard

Spratt, Sarah, dry goods' store, btw Vir and Ls N Yard

Spratt, Thomas, tavern, e side 9w btw Pen av and Dn

Sprigg, Benjamin, clk in office of the clerk H. of Representatives; dw w side 1e btw B and Cn Cap Hill

Sprigg, Thomas B. (col. man) pump borer, e side 12w btw E and Fn

Spooner, Mrs. Ls btw 4 and 5e N Yard

Stakelberg, The Baron, Swedish charge des affaires; dw n side Pen av btw 18 and 19w

Stansbury, Arthur Joseph, stenographer, e side N Jer av btw B and Cs Cap Hill

Stanley, Thomas, painter, n side Pen av btw 9 and 10w

Stanley, Thomas B. brickmaker, e side N Jer av btw K & Ls

Stanwell, William, carpenter, n side Dn btw 12 and 13w

Staughton, James M., M. D. s side Fn btw 11 and 12w

Steiner, John C. clk register's office; dw Georgetown

Stephens, Edward, clk secretary war's office; dw 14w btw F and Gn

Stettinius, John, dry goods' store, n side Pen av btw 6 & 7w

Stettinius, Samuel, grocer, corner Pen av and Cn

Stevens, Thomas Holdup, master commandant at N Yard; dw in the yard

Steveson, John, grocer, s side East Cap st opposite market, Capitol Hill

Stevenson, Wesley, grocer, w side 7w btw G and Hn

Stevenson, Mr. 7w near the Potomac

Steuart, William, clk 2d auditor's office; dw Georgetown

Stewart, William M. clk sec'y war's office

Stewart, James, brickmaker, 1e btw L and Ms

Stewart, Walter 12w btw C and Dn

Stewart, John, carpenter, n side East Cap st opp market, Capitol Hill

Stewart, Eliza, boarding house, 11w btw Pen av and En

Stewart, Gen. Philip, 4½w btw N and Os Greenleaf's Point

Stewart, William H. bricklayer, n e corner En and 11w

Stewart, Samuel, messenger, w side 11w btw G and Hn

Stewart, David, coachmaker, Pen av west of and near the Capitol

Steward, William, carter, w side 11w near Tiber creek

Stewart, Charles I. carter, w side 12w btw G and Hn

Stephens, Jemima, (col. woman) w side 7w btw Lou av & Du

Stewart, James, (col. man) hackman, 15w btw H and In

Steuart, Charles, (col. man) Pen av btw 17 and 18w

Steuart, Charles, (col. man) waiter, corner 15w and Nn

Stickney, Mary Ann, widow, s e corner I s and 10e N Yard

Stisie, Leonard, cabinet maker, Gn btw 17 and 18w

Stillins, John, cabinet maker, Vir av btw 7 and 8e N Yard

Stinchcomb, Noah, carpenter, w side 7w btw H and In

Stinchcomb, Aquila, 7e btw L and Ms N Yard

Stinger, Frederick, clerk at glass works

Stone, William J. engraver and copperplate printer, n side Pen av btw 12 and 13w

Stowers, Mrs. female academy, 12w btw E and Fn

Stockwell, John, printer, w side 11w btw E and Fn

Stras, Martha, widow, Pen av btw 13 and 14w

Stretch, John, clk register's office; dw Georgetown

Strother, John, e side 14w btw Pen av and Fn

Street, John, grocer, s side Gn btw 18 and 19w

Strickland, Catharine, widow, 4e btw K and Ls

Stubbs, Thomas, drayman, w side N Jer av btw L and Ms

Suit, John, laborer, Ls btw 7 and 8e Navy Yard

Sullivan, Mary, mantuamaker, s side Fn btw 11 and 12w

Sullivan, Jeremiah, tavernkeeper, e side 7w btw G and Hn

Summers, O. saddler, 7w btw F and Gn

Susock, S. grocer, corner 12w and Gn

Sutton, Thomas, blacksmith, G.. av w 11 and 12e N Yard

Sutton, Samuel, butcher, Gn btw 18 and w

Suter, Alexander, clk Farmers and Mechanics' bank; dw near Georgetown low   d e

Suter, John, clk gen post office; dw n side Fn btw 13 & 14w

Swann, Thomas, district attorney; dw Hn fronting President's square

Swan, M. potter, 7e btw L and Ms Navy Yard

Sweeney, George, ch clk city post office; dw 7w btw D & En

Sweeney, William H. laborer, 13½w btw D and En

Sweeney, Edward, grocer, East Capitol st opposite market, Capitol Hill

Sweeney, James, grocer, 1e btw A and Bs Cap Hill

Symonson, Lieut. James, commandant at the arsenal, Greenleaf's Point

T.

TABLER, JOHN, tailor, e side 10w btw D and En

Taffa, Ann, widow, 8e btw Vir av and I s. N Yard

Taitt, Alexander, stonecutter, A s. fronting Capitol square, Capitol Hill

Talbot, Thomas, shipcarpenter, Ks btw 11 and 12e N Yard

Talbot, Ellen, e side 8e near marine barracks, N Yard

Talburt, A. grocer, e side 7w btw G and Hn

Tarlton, Merritt, Cn btw 6 and 7w

Tastet, N. clk gen post office; dw En btw 10 and 11w

Tate, Andrew,   ditto   dw s side Dn btw 6 and 7w

Taylor, Jos.   ditto   dw 7w btw I and Kn

Taylor, John, bricklayer, near the glass house

Taylor, jun. Thomas, wood corder, dw ditto

Taylor, Joseph, dw   ditto

Taylor, Richard, shoemaker, 7e btw F and Gs N Yard

Taylor, George, Bn btw 1 and 2e Cap Hill

Taylor, Mrs. Rebecca, 9w near En

Taylor, Parnell B. blacksmith, Ms btw 5 and 6w

Taylor, George, e side 19w btw F and Gn

Taylor, jun. George, teacher, 20w btw H and Pen av

Taylor, Robert, captain steamboat Metropolis; dw s side En btw 12 and 13w

Tayloe, Col. John, corner N York av and 18w
Teachem, Henry, 3e btw M and Ns
Tebbs, Thomas, M. D. 21w near Pen avenue
Tennison, Joshua, w side 10w btw D and En
Tennison, George, proprietor of the Washington Coffee
House, w side 10w btw D and En
Tench, James, laborer, Ls btw 8 and 9e Navy Yard
Thaw, Joseph, clk 5th auditor's office; dw 7 buildings
Thompson, James, ch clk 3d auditor's office; dw corner
Mn and 24w
Thompson, Pishey, bookseller, n side Pen av btw 11 & 12w
Thompson, Allen, printer, 12w btw Pen av and Cn
Thompson, Robert, saddler, 6w btw Pen av and Cn
Thompson, John L. carpenter, near corner 20w and New
York avenue
Thompson, Archibald, bricklayer, Fn btw 18 and 19w
Thompson, Richard, tailor, (firm of Tucker and Thomp-
son;) dw w side 12w btw G and Hn
Thompson, Margaret, widow, corner Dn and 14w
Thompson, B 26w near the Georgetown upper bridge
Thompson, James, blockmaker, Geo av near navy yard
Thompson, William, cabinet maker, corner Pen av and 15w
Thompson, Edward, bricklayer, South Cap st btw C and Ds
Capitol Hill
Thompson, Joseph, blacksmith, Ls btw 3e and N Jer av
Thompson, William, shipcarpenter, Ls btw 6 and 7e N Yard
Thompson, Arthur, printer, n side Hn near 7w
Thomas, Robert, South Capitol st near Eastern branch
Thomas, Thomas, blacksmith, Ks near Eastern branch
Thomas, Ann, e side 8w btw G and Hn
Thornton, Dr. William, superintendent patent office; dw
n side Fn btw 13 and 14w
Thornton, Dolly, (col) washerwoman, 26w btw I and Kn
Thruston, Buckner, judge circuit court; dw s side Bs btw
N Jer av and 1e Cap Hill

Thruston, Thomas L clk secretary state's office; dw N Jer
   av near bank of Washington
Thumblert William, shoemaker, n side Pen av near Indian
   Queen hotel; dw Cn btw 4½ and 6w
Ticer, Thomas, tavernkeeper, 12w near Tiber creek
Tilley, Ann, widow, 20w near western market
Tilghman, Rebecca, (col.) washerwoman, 3e near Md av
Tims, Henry, doorkeeper of the senate; dw A s. fronting
   the Capitol square
Tims Charles, apothecary and druggist; dw ditto
Tingey, Com. Thomas, navy commissioner
Tinney, Charles, 1w near old tanyard
Tippett, Edward D. teacher, w side N Jer av btw I and Ks
Tippett, John, 3e btw I s. and Vir avenue
Tippett, Maximilian, turnkey at the prison; dw Fn btw
   2 and 3w
Todd, S. I. and Co. druggists, n side Pen av btw 6 and 7w
Tonge, Richard, tinman, Pen av btw 11 and 12w
Tool, Peter, blacksmith, Fs btw 7 and 8e Navy Yard
Torrence, James, porter cellar, 15w near treasury dep't
Townsend, L. n w corner 7e and I s. Navy Yard
Towson, Col. Nathan, paymaster general; dw corner Fn &
   17w near war department
Townley, James, Pen av btw 14 and 15w
Travers, Miss Sidney, n side Pen av btw 12 and 13w
Travers, Esias, baker, dw   ditto
Travers, Capt. George, corner South Cap st and Ns
Travis, Levin, waterman, w side 3e btw M and Ns
Trammell, Mary, near Mn and Georgetown upper bridge
Trehorn, James, tailor, 10 buildings
Tree, Lambert, messenger gen post office; dw Fn near 7w
Trimble, Matthew, grocer, s w corner I s. and 8e N Yard
Triplett, Thomas, 16w btw I and Kn
Tschiffely, Lewis S. clk in register's office; dw Gn btw
   17 and 18w

Tucker, Thomas T. treasurer of the U. States; at T. B Dashieli's, 1 n. and 18w

Tucker, Mrs. widow, boarding house, s w corner Pen av and 10w

Tucker and Thompson, merchant tailors, s side Pen av opp National hotel

Tucker, Samuel, brickmaker, 14e near Eastern branch

Tucker, Elizabeth, widow, btw 5 and 6e near Md avenue

Turner, John, carpenter, w side 6w btw F and Gn

Turner, Daniel, stonecutter, 1e btw A and Bs Cap Hill

Turner, John, laborer, Bn btw 6 and 7w

Turton, Ferdinand, grocer, Pen av btw 17 and 18w

Tweedy, Robert, messenger of the Senate, n w corner of Gn and 12w

Tyler, B. O. lottery office, two doors east of Indian Queen hotel; dw A n. fronting Capitol square

Tyler, Charles, clk gen land office; dw extreme boundary of the city, north of the capitol

Tyler, Edward, (col. man) laborer, Cs btw 2 and 3e

U.

UNDERHILL, LEVI, carpenter, w side 13½w near the Tiber

Underwood, John, clk 1st auditor's office; dw Missouri av btw 3 and 4½w

Upton, Thomas, laborer, 10e opposite Navy Yard

Ustick, Stephen C. printer, n side Dn near Pairo's dry goods' store; dw s side Dn near corner 10w

V.

VAIL, MRS. widow, 7 buildings, Pen avenue

Vail, Aaron, clk secretary state's office; dw ditto

Vail, Eugene A. clk gen land office; dw   ditto

Vail, Thomas, blacksmith, Union st Greenleaf's Point

Vallitt, Elizabeth, widow, washerwoman, 14w btw Pen av
   and Tiber creek
Van Coble, Aaron, carpenter, s side Cn btw 4½ and 6w
Van Horn, Jeremiah, boatbuilder at navy yard; dw Ks btw
   10 and 11e Navy Yard
Van Ness, Gen John P. president bank of Metropolis; dw
   17w near the river
Van Reswick, John, 4½w btw N and Os Greenleaf''s Point
Van Reswick, Wilford, joinef, 3e btw M and Ns
Vanscomb, John, Geo av btw 9 and 10e N Yard
Vanzandt, Nicholas B land agent, Pen av east of and near
   Capitol square, Capitol Hill
Varnum, Jacob B. corner Lou av and 8w
Vaughan, Hon. Charles Richard, minister plenipotentiary
   from Great Britain ; near western market
Veitch, Barbara, widow, s side Bs btw 1 and 2e Cap Hill
Venable, George, tinman, n w corner I s. and 11e N Yard
Venable, Joseph, s e corner 4e and Ls
Venable, Charles, tinman, n side Pen av btw 7 and 8e
Vermillion, Otho T. tailor, Ls btw 7 and 8e N Yard
Vermillion, Levi, laborer, s side Bs btw 1e and N Jer av
   Capitol Hill
Vermillion, Dennis, shipcarpenter, 5e near Eastern branch,
   Navy Yard
Vinson, Charles, clk 3d auditor's office; dw I n. near 18w
Vivan, Louis, tavernkeeper, corner Pen av and 17w

W.

WADE, JOHN H. printer, w side 10w btw G and Hn
Wade, Major W. clk ordnance department; dw Fn near the
   war office
Wadsworth, Captain Alexander A. Ps btw 4½ and Potomac,
   Greenleaf's Point
Wagler, F. A. professor of music, Hn btw 17 and 18w

Wailes, I. H. hat store, one door west of Mansion hotel

Wailes, Dorothy, w side N Jer av btw K and Ls

Wailes, Thomas, blacksmith, 20 buildings, South Cap st

Waite, Matthew, slater, 3w near Pen avenue

Walker, Samuel P. merchant, s w corner Pen av and 11w; dw opposite Mansion hotel, Pen avenue

Walker, Charles, captain steamboat Mount Vernon, Es btw 10 and 11w

Walker, William B. coach painter, 13w btw C and Dn

Walker, Rosanna, w side 8e near barracks, N Yard

Walker, Singleton S. clk at National Journal office

Walker, Zachariah, pumpmaker, 13w btw C and Dn

Walker, George, and son James, butchers, 1 n btw 18 & 19w

Wallack, Richard, attorney at law, s side Lou av near the City hall

Wallace, James, clk to attorney general, Fn near 12w

Wallace, William, constable, s side Hn btw 6 and 7w

Waller, A. Bradley, china store, n side Lou av btw 7 and 8w; dw 7w btw D and En

Wannells, Thomas, shoemaker, s side Pen av btw 9 and 10w

Warrington, Capt. Lewis, navy commissioner; dw s side Fn opposite bank of Metropolis

Ward, William, dry goods' store, n side Pen av near Indian Queen hotel

Ward, Michael, grocery, s e corner Cn and 12w

Waring, Basil, clk 5th auditor's office; dw N York av west of navy department

Warren, Joseph, messenger, corner 15w and Kn

Warner, Elizabeth, n side Pen av btw 2 and 3w

Warner, Samuel, blockmaker, Geo av Navy Yard

Warner, Thomas, s side Es btw 9 and 10w

Washington, Peter G. clk secretary of treasury's office; dw Greenleaf's Point

Washington, Lund, clk 1st comptroller's office; dw 14w btw F and Gn

8

Washington, Sarah, widow, w side 12w btw Pen av and Em

Washington, Amelia, (col.) washerwoman, Pen av btw 17 and 18w

Washburn, Levi, grocer, s side Pen av btw 21 and 22w

Wason, Edward, blacksmith, 7e btw F and Gs N Yard

Watson, Col. Joseph, military and general land and tax ag't, s side Pen av btw 9 and 10w; dw at Mrs. Blake's, corner Lou av and 8w

Watson, Andrew J. clk 1st auditor's office; dw corner Gn and 19w

Watson, Alexander R. assistant messenger treasury dept. dw Lou av btw 6 and 7w

Watson, Alexander, 13w near Dn

Watkins, Mrs. widow, Ms btw 9 and 10e N Yard

Watkins, Dr. Tobias, 4th auditor; dw n w corner I n & 17

Watkins, George, clk department of state; dw ditto

Watson, James, asst. messenger register's office; dw near the war office

Watson, James W. schoolmaster, 7e btw L and Ms N Yard

Watterston, George, librarian of Congress library; dw 2e btw Pen av and Cs Capitol Hill

Waters, William, magistrate, n side Pen av btw 19 and 20w

Waters, John, Mn btw 17 and 18w

Waters, John, police officer, 10w btw G and Hn

Watters, Benjamin, lumber merchant, near centre market; dw at Alexandria

Wathen, Thomas, laborer, s side East Capitol st btw 3 & 4e

Wathen, William, laborer, Ls btw 4 and 5e

Way and Gideon, printers and bookbinders, w side 9w btw Pen av and Dn

Way, Andrew, (firm of Way and Gideon,) n side Pen av btw 9 and 10w

Weavear, John, painter and glazier, Gn btw 18 and 19w

Weaver, James, (col. man) shoemaker, w side N Jer av btw L and Ms

Webb, John F. lottery and exchange broker, n side Pen av corner National hotel; dw s side Lou av near Theatre

Webster, Samuel, clk 1st comptr's office; dw Georgetown

Weed, Lieut. Elijah J. quartermaster marine corps, at the barracks, N Yard

Weightman, Roger C. cashier of the bank of Washington; dw e side N Jer av btw B and Cs Cap Hill

Weightman, Henry T. cashier of the Patriotic bank; dw at the bank

Wells, jr. John, book keeper 2d auditor's office; dw 16w btw I and Kn

Wells, Richard, grocer, s side Pen av btw 12 and 13w

Wells, Samuel, carpenter, w side 7w btw H and I n

Wells, Richard, laborer, 12w btw C and Dn

Welsh, Thomas, Dn 2d door east of Unitarian church

Wertz, Mrs. boarding house, Pen av btw 2 and 3e

Westcott, Ann, widow, near the old tanyard, Vir av

Westerfield, David, cabinet maker, s side Pen av btw 3 & 4½w

Wharton, Charles H. W. magistrate; office opp gen post office; dw En btw 13 and 14w

Wharton, Lemuel, Ns near N Jer av

Wheat, Thomas, teacher, corner 6e and I s N Yard

Wheat, Rachel, widow, east side 3e near Eastern branch

Wheat, William, opposite N Yard market

Wheat, John, gardener, 4½w btw N & Os Greenleaf's Point

Wheatly, Ignatius, laborer, n w corner Fn and 2w

Wheaton, Joseph, s side Fn btw 13 and 14w

Whetcroft, Henry, clk 3d auditor's office; dw s side Fn btw 17 and 18w

White, Levi, grocer, Ls btw 4 and 5e Navy Yard

White, Charles, shoemaker, w side N Jer av btw 1 and 2e

White, Elijah, tinman, n side Pen av btw 10 and 11w

White, Gilbert, stonemason, 11w btw Md av and Es

White, Matilda, widow, n side Pen av btw 1 and 2w

White, Wm. G. dry goods' store, s side Pen av btw 6 & 7w

White, Thomas, shipcarpenter, Ks btw 10 and 11e N Yard

White, Ambrose, bricklayer, South Capitol st btw C and D's
  Capitol Hill

White, Mr. millwright, 26w btw I and Kn

Whittemore, Edward, blacksmith, Ns near N Jer av

Whitaker, J. Thos. printer, n side Fn near Catholic church

Wigley, Ann, widow, n e corner 10c and Ks N Yard

Wilcox, Eleanor, widow, Eastern branch upper bridge

Wilcox, Charles W. clk commissary gen of subsistence

Williams, Elizabeth, widow, Lou av btw 6 and 7w

Williams, Elizabeth, widow, Vir av btw 7 and 8e N Yard

Williams, Brooke, clk adjt gen's office; dw Georgetown

Williams, Jeremiah, clk 1st auditor's office; dw   ditto

Williams, George W. shoemaker, 8w btw Pen av and Dn

Williams, William, shoemaker, n side Dn btw 6 and 7w

Williams, Philip, grocer, I n opposite western market

Williams, John and James, cabinet makers, n side Pen av
  btw 17 and 18w

Williams, Zedekiah, laborer, 5e btw K and Ls N Yard

Williamson, William, clk in first comptroller's office; dw
  Georgetown

Williamson, Bazil, proprietor Mansion hotel, Pen av btw 14
  and 15w

Williamson, Benjamin, carpenter, s w corner En and 11w

Wilbour, Elizabeth, widow, 8e btw Vir av and I s N Yard

Wilburn, Rezin, laborer, 8e btw I and Ks Navy Yard

Williss, William, laborer, Ls btw 8 and 9e N Yard

Wilson, Mary, widow, bd'ng house, n side Fn btw 11 & 12w

Wilson, Elizabeth, widow, n side Fn btw 11 and 12w

Wilson, Thomas L. printer, e side 9w btw D and Fn

Wilson, James, printer, 5w near Fn

Wilson, Thomas, carpenter, 17w opposite the war office

Wilson, John A. n side Gn btw 14 and 15w

Wilson, D. M. hatter, n side Pen av btw 9 and 10w; dw
  south side, opposite.

Wilson, Charles, gardener, Md av btw 6 and 7w

Wilson, John, s side Pen av btw 18 and 19w

Wilson, Catharine, spinster, I s near 1½w

Wilson, Ann, (col.) washerwoman, near corner 16w and Ln

Wilstach, Charles F., M. D. chemist and apothecary, n side Pen av btw 9 and 10w

Wiltberger, Charles H. clk to the mayor and register, west wing city hall; dw corner 13w and Cn

Wimsatt, Samuel, wood corder and coal measurer, 11w btw D and Es

Winn, Timothy, purser at navy yard; dw I s btw 10 & 11e Navy Yard

Windham, Mary, spinster, s w corner 17w and I n

Wineberger, Jacob, baker, 28w near Georgetown Pr bridge

Wirt, William, attorney general of the U. States, s side Gn btw 17 and 18w

Wiseman, John, 1e near the Eastern branch

Wise, William, laborer, Union st Greenleaf's Point

Wolfenden, J. apothecary, n e corner En and 7w

Wood, Joseph, miniature painter, n side Pen av btw 9 & 10w

Wood, George, clk gen land office; dw 14w north of Methodist church

Wood, William, tavernkeeper, A s. fronting the Capitol square, Capitol Hill

Wood, John, btw 11 and 12e and L and Ms N Yard

Woodward, William, printer, Fn btw 6 and 7w

Woodward, Amon, city pump maker, s side En btw 12 and 13w

Woodside, James D. clk in register's office; dw 19w btw I and Kn

Woodside, John, clk 1st comptroller's office; dw 6 buildings, Pen avenue

Wormly, William, (col.) hackman, I n btw 15 and 16w

Wright, Matthew, n w corner I s and 8e N Yard

Wright, Richard, auctioneer, n side Pen av btw 9 and 10w; dw s e corner Dn and 8w

Wright, James, grocer, corner Md av and 2e Cap Hill

8*

Wright, Nathaniel, carpenter, n side En btw 10 and 11w

Wright, James, barber, 1 n opposite western market

Wroe, Absalom, grocer, e side 7w btw G and Hn

Y.

YATEMAN, MRS. e side 10w btw D and En

Young, William, saddler, n side Gn btw 14 and 15w

Young, James, grocery, s e corner N Jer av and Bs, dw
N Jer av btw B and Cs Capitol Hill

Young, Thomas, shipcarpenter, s w corner Ms and 11e
Navy Yard

Young, Abner, tailor, w side 10w btw E and Fn

Young, E. and A. H. merchant tailors, n side Pen av btw
10 and 11w

Young, David, butcher, s e corner 16w and Ln

Young, Ezekiel, merchant tailor, n side Pen av btw 9 & 10w

Young, John, butcher, e side 13w btw E and Fn

CHARTER OF WASHINGTON.

Abstract of the Act of Incorporation, or Charter, of the City, Passed by Congress, 15th May, 1820.

Sec. 1. In this section, all former acts of incorporation are declared to be repealed. It provides, however, that the Members of the Corporation in office at the time of the passage of this act are to continue as such until the expiration of the terms for which they were respectively appointed; and all their acts done in pursuance of former acts of incorporation, and not inconsistent with this one, are to remain valid.

Sec. 2, Enacts that the inhabitants of Washington shall continue to be a body politic and corporate, by the name of the "Mayor, Board of Aldermen, and Board of Common Council, of the City of Washington;" and, by their corporate name, are authorized to do all acts as natural persons; and that they may have a city seal, which they may alter at pleasure.

Sec. 3, Declares that the Mayor shall be elected biennially, commencing on the first Monday in June, 1820, at the same time and place, in the same manner, and by the persons qualified to vote for the Boards of Aldermen and Common Council. Commissioners of Election are to make out duplicate certificates of the result of the election, and return one to each Board on the Monday following the election; and the person having the greatest number of votes shall be the Mayor: but in case two or more, highest in vote, shall have an equal number, then the Boards are to determine, by ballot in joint meeting, the choice between them. The Mayor must, on the Monday ensuing his election, take an oath in presence of the two Boards, to be administered by a justice of the peace, " lawfully to execute the duties of his office, to the best of his skill and judgment, without favor or partiality." By virtue of his office, he is to be a justice of the peace for the county of Washington. He is empowered, with the consent of the Board of Aldermen, to appoint all officers under the corporation, (except commissioners of election,) and may remove them at pleasure. He may appoint persons to fill vacancies which occur during the recess of said Board, to hold their offices until the end of the then ensuing session. He may convene the two Boards when in his opinion the public good may require it; he shall lay before them in writing such alterations in the laws of the corporation as he may deem proper; and he shall receive for his services, annually, a compensation, which shall not be altered during his continuation in office. Any person is eligible to the office of Mayor, who is a free white male citizen, thirty years of age, has been a resident of the city for two years preceding the election, and who is the bona fide owner of a freehold estate in the city. In case of the refusal of the Mayor elect to accept of the office, or of his death, resignation, inability, or removal, the said Boards shall elect another, to serve for the remainder of the term, or during such inability.

SEC. 4, Enacts that the Board of Aldermen shall consist of two members to be residents in and chosen from each ward, by the qualified voters therein, to be elected for two years from the Monday next ensuing their election. The Board of Common Council shall consist of three members from each ward, to be chosen in like manner, for one year. Each board shall meet at the council chamber, at ten o'clock, on the second Monday in June in every year, and at such other times as they may by law direct. A majority of each Board is necessary to form a quorum; but a less number may adjourn from day to day. They may compel the attendance of absent members; and regulate their own compensation. Each Board to choose its own President, who is entitled to a vote. They shall fix their rules of proceeding, choose their own officers, regulate their compensations, and remove them at pleasure. They may, three fourths concurring, expel any member for disorderly behaviour or malconduct in office, but not a second time for the second offence. Each Board shall keep a journal of its proceedings, and the yeas and nays shall be entered thereon at the request of any member. Their deliberations shall be public. All their ordinances or acts shall be sent to the Mayor, and, if approved by him, shall be obligatory. But if the Mayor does not approve of any ordinance or act, he shall return it within five days, with the reasons, in writing, of his disapproval; but if, on a reconsideration, two-thirds of both Boards agree to pass the same, it shall be valid. If the Boards, by their adjournment, prevent its return, it shall not be obligatory.

Sec. 5, Designates the qualifications of members of the two boards, and of voters. No person is eligible to a seat in either board, unless he is upwards of twenty-five, a free white male citizen, has resided in the city for one year next preceding the election, is a resident of the ward for which he is

elected, the bona fide owner of a freehold estate in
the city, and shall have been assessed on the books
of the corporation for the year ending on the 31st
of December next preceding the election.   Voters
must be in like manner qualified, except that it is
not requisite for them to own a freehold estate,
nor to be more .than twenty-one; voters, must,
however, in addition to the above qualifications,
have paid all taxes legally assessed and due on personal property, when legally required to pay the
same, before they can exercise the right of suffrage.
It is enjoined upon the City Register, or such person as the corporation may direct, to furnish the
oommissioners of election in each ward, previous
to every election, with a list of the persons having
a right to vote.

SEC. 6, Requires an election for members of the
two boards to be held on the first Monday in June,
annually.   Three commissioners are to be appointed for each ward, by the boards in joint meeting,
ten days at least before the election.   It shall be the
duty of the commissioners to give at least five
days' notice of the places where the election is to
be held.   They are to take an oath "truly and
faithfully to receive and return the votes of such
persons as are by law entitled to vote for members
of the two boards in their respective wards; and
not knowingly to receive or return the vote of any
person who is not legally entitled to the same."
The polls shall be opened at ten in the morning,
and close at seven in the evening.   As soon as the
polls are closed, the commissioners shall make out
a correct return of the persons having the greatest
number of legal votes for members of the two
boards, respectively, together with the number of
votes for each person voted for.   The persons ha-

ing the greatest number of votes, shall be duly
elected; and in all cases of an equality, the commissioners shall decide the choice by lot. The said
returns shall be made to the Mayor on the day suc-
ceeding the election, who shall cause them to be
published. A duplicate return, together with a list
of the persons who voted, shall also be made at the
same time to the City Register, who shall record
the same ; and shall, within two days thereafter,
notify the several persons returned of their election.
Each board shall judge of the legality of the elections of its own members, and shall supply vacancies in its own body, by causing elections to fill the
same, and appointing commissioners who are to
give the usual notice of the time and place of hold-
ing such elections. The members of either board
shall take an oath or affirmation, "faithfully to execute the duties of his office to the best of his know-
ledge and ability," to be administered by the Mayor, or a justice of the peace.

Sec. 7, Defines the powers of the Corporation.
They are authorized to tax all real and personal
property, provided said tax does not exceed three-
fourths per cent. on the assessment, except for
special purposes; wearing apparel, or the necessary tools and implements used in carrying on the
trade or occupation of any person, not to be taxed,
nor subject to seizure for taxes; after providing
for all objects of a general nature, the balance of
taxes to be expended in the ward where raised.
The corporation shall have power to establish a
board of health, who shall have authority to enforce its regulations, and take measures to prevent
the introduction of contagious diseases; prevent
and remove nuisances; establish night watches;
erect lamps; preserve the navigation of the rivers;

erect and regulate public wharves: deepen creeks, docks, and basins; regulate the manner of erecting private wharves, and their rates of wharfage; the stationing of vessels; provide for licensing, taxing, and regulating auctions, retailers, ordinaries, and taverns, carriages, wagons, carts, and drays, pawn brokers, venders of lottery tickets, money changers, and hawkers and pedlars; theatrical or public shows; tippling houses, lotteries, and all kinds of gaming; regulate and establish markets; erect bridges; open and keep in repair streets and drains, agreeably to the plan of the city; supply water; provide for the safe keeping of the standard weights and measures, as fixed by Congress, and regulate those used in the city; regulate the sweeping of chimneys, and the fees therefor; provide for the prevention and extinguishment of fires; regulate the size of bricks; provide for the inspection of lumber, and other building materials; and, with the approbation of the President of the United States, to regulate the manner of erecting, and the materials to be used in the erection of, houses; regulate the inspection of country produce, and salted provisions; the gauging of casks and liquors; the storage of gunpowder and all naval and military stores, not the property of the United States; to impose and appropriate fines, &c. for the breach of their laws; and to provide for the appointment of the officers necessary to execute the laws of the Corporation.

SEC. 8, Further empowers the Corporation to tax particular wards, or parts, for their local improvement; and, upon application of the owners of more than one half of the property upon any portion of a street, to cause the curb stones to be set and the foot-way to be paved, on such portion, and to tax such property to the amount of the expense thereof, provided said tax shall not exceed three dollars per front foot. Upon like application, they may cause the carriage-way to be paved, or lamps erected, the expense to be defrayed by the imposition of a tax on the lot fronting the portion so improved; and if said tax is not paid within thirty days after it becomes due, an interest at the rate of ten per cent. per annum, may be demanded. The corporation is authorized to establish, superintend, and endow, public schools; all necessary public institutions and buildings, and impose taxes to defray the expense thereof; regulate party walls and fences, and determine by whom they shall be kept in repair; cause new alleys to be opened, and extend those already laid out, in any square, upon application of the owners of more than half of the property in such square; but it is provided, that if any individual suffers damage, he shall be indemnified therefor by the corporation, after the amount shall have been ascertained by a jury summoned by the marshal; the amount of damages, and the expenses accruing, to be levied upon the property benefitted. They are empowered to improve, for public purposes, with the consent of the President, any public ground, not interfering with private rights; regulate the admeasurement and weight by which all articles for sale shall be disposed of; provide for the appointment of appraisers and measurers of builders' work and materials, and of wood, coal, grain, and lumber; restrain the disorderly meetings of slaves, free negroes, and mulattoes, and punish such slaves by whipping, not exceeding forty stripes, or by imprisonment, not exceeding six months, for one offence; and to punish such free negroes and mu-

9

lattoes by penalties not exceeding twenty dollars for one offence, and in case of their inability, to confine them not exceeding six months; and they may cause all vagrants, disorderly or suspicious persons, eves-droppers, and night-walkers, gamblers, prostitutes, and all who lead an immoral course of life, to give security for their good behaviour, and to indemnify the city against any charge for their support, and if they do not give such security, to confine them to labor, not exceeding one year at a time; to bind out poor orphans, and the children of vagrants, and paupers; prescribe the terms upon which free negroes and mulattoes may reside in the city; authorize, with the approbation of the President of the United States, the drawing of lotteries for making those improvements in the city which the ordinary revenue will not accomplish, for ten years, provided the amount so raised shall not exceed ten thousand dollars in any one year, clear of expenses; to regulate burying grounds; provide for the registering of births, deaths, and marriages; to punish colored servants or slaves, for a breach of their laws, unless the master of such servants or slaves shall pay the fine; and they may pass all laws which may be deemed necessary to carry into execution the powers vested by this act in said Corporation.

Sec. 9, Makes it the duty of the Marshal of the District of Columbia, to keep within the jail for the County of Washington, all persons committed thereto, by authority of this act; and where suits shall be had before a justice of the peace, for the recovery of fines, by the Corporation, executions shall be issued, as in other cases of small debts.

Sec. 10, Authorizes the sale by auction of real property, on which two years' taxes are due, or so much thereof as may be necessary to pay such taxes, and costs; public notice thereof to be given in some newspaper of the city, once a week for six months, when the property is assessed to persons residing out of the United States; for three months when they reside in the United States, but out of the District; and for six weeks when they reside in the District; which advertisement shall describe the property, give the person's name to whom assessed, and the amount of taxes due thereon. The purchaser to pay at the time of sale, the amount of taxes and expenses, and the residue within two years and ten days from the sale, which shall be placed in the city treasury and remain subject to the order of the original proprietor; the purchaser to receive from the Mayor a title in fee simple. It is provided that the proprietor may redeem his property so sold, within two years, by paying or tendering to the purchaser, or depositing with the Mayor, and notifying the purchaser thereof, the amount paid by the purchaser, and ten per cent. per annum thereon. If the purchaser fails to pay the residue within the two years and ten days, he shall pay an interest thereon of ten per cent. per annum, until he does pay it, and receive a conveyance from the Corporation; the interest, like the residue, to be subject to the order of the original proprietor. No sale is to be made of improved property, whereon there is personal property sufficient to pay the taxes; minors, mortgagees, and others, having equitable interests in real property sold for taxes, are allowed one year after such minors coming of age, or the others, have obtained a decree for its sale, to redeem the property so sold, which they may do by paying to the purchaser a sum equal to the whole amount he has paid on said property up to the period of redemption, with ten per cent. interest, and also the full value of the improvements thereon made by the purchaser. Where the estate of the tenant in default, as for years, or life, is sufficient to pay the taxes, such estate only shall be sold.

SEC. 11, Makes it lawful for the collector to postpone the sale, for want of bidders, he giving public notice thereof, and the sale made at such postponed time is to be as valid as if made on the day first stated.

SEC. 12, Authorizes the collector to proceed by distress and sale of goods and chattels, in the collection of all legal taxes, after giving ten days' notice in a newspaper of the city. The laws of Maryland relative to the right of replevying, are made applicable to cases of personal property taken by distress for taxes imposed by the Corporation.

SEC. 13, Declares that the Levy Court of Washington County shall not have the power of taxing property in the city. The Corporation are exempted from contributing towards defraying the expenses of said court, except for one half incurred on account of the orphans' court, the office of coroner, the county jail, and the opening and repairing of roads east of Rock creek, leading to the city; but the corporation are to have the sole control of the bridge over Rock creek, at the termination of K street north, which they must repair and rebuild when necessary.

SEC. 14, Requires the clerk of the Circuit Court, and the register of wills, for the county of Washington, respectively, to furnish the city register with semi-annual lists of the transfers of real property in the city; for which service the said clerk and register of wills are to be paid not exceeding six cents for each transfer.

SEC. 15, Authorizes and requires the commissioner of the public buildings to reimburse to the corporation a just proportion of the expenses incurred in opening, paving, or improving, any of the streets which pass by the United States' squares or reservations; which proportion shall be determined by a comparison of the length of their front with the whole extent of their two sides; and the commissioner shall cause the foot ways to be paved in front of any square, reservation, or lot, belonging to the United States, whenever the corporation shall direct the like improvements to be made on the opposite or adjoining squares or lots. The expenses to be defrayed by the commissioner out of moneys arising from the sale of United States' lots in the city.

SEC. 16, Authorizes the boards of aldermen and common council, from time to time, to divide the city into as many wards as they think proper, provided that each ward shall comprise, as near as may be, an equal number of inhabitants.* Expenses incurred in improving the streets which form the boundaries of the wards, to be defrayed out of the taxes raised in the wards which adjoin them, in equal proportions. The corporation is required, before the first Monday in June, 1820, to apportion amongst the wards hereby established, such portions of the city debt as have heretofore been chargeable to the old wards. The board of alder-

---

* This section divides the city into six wards; but the necessity of defining their limits here is superseded, as the Corporation, on the 24th May, 1820. by virtue of the power vested in them to that effect, have made a new division,— See Map of the City.

men are directed, on the second Monday in June,
1820, as soon as organized, to divide themselves
into two classes, as follow: Those members now
in office, and, by virtue of their election in June,
1819, are entitled to take their seats in the new
board as members from the wards in which they
shall reside, shall be placed in the first class; those
members who shall be elected from the same
wards, in June next, shall be placed in the second
class; and the other members shall be placed in
their respective classes by lot; the seats of the first
class to be vacated at the end of the first year, and
the seats of the second class at the end of the second year; so that one member shall be elected
in each ward every year thereafter. Aldermen
are to be, by virtue of their office, justices of the
peace for the county of Washington, unless hold-
ing commissions in the army or navy of the United
States.

SEC. 17, Declares that this act shall continue in
force for twenty years, and until Congress shall
determine otherwise.

AN ACT

Amendatory of the Charter of the City of Washington.

AN ACT supplementary to the act "to incorporate the
inhabitants of the City of Washington," passed the fifteenth of May, one thousand eight hundred and twenty,
and for other purposes.

*Be it enacted by the Senate and House of
Representatives of the United States of America
in Congress assembled,* That so much of the act,
entitled "An act to incorporate the inhabitants of

the city of Washington, and to repeal all acts heretofore passed for that purpose," passed May the fifteenth, one thousand eight hundred and twenty, as is inconsistent with the provisions of this act, be, and the same is hereby repealed.

Sec. 2. *And be it further enacted,* That public notice of the time and place of the sale of all real property, for taxes due the Corporation of the city of Washington, shall be given in all cases hereafter, by advertisement, inserted in some newspaper published in the said city, once in each week, for at least twelve successive weeks, in which advertisement shall be stated the number of the square or squares, the number of the lot or lots, (if the square has been divided into lots,) the name or names of the person or persons to whom the same may be assessed on the books of the Corporation at the time of such advertisement, the amount of the tax due on each square or lot, the period for which the same shall be due, and the aggregate amount of taxes due on all real property assessed in the name of the same person or persons; but, where a whole square is assessed to the same person or persons, although divided into lots, it may be assessed and advertised, as if the same was not divided. And no sale of real property, for taxes, hereafter made, shall be impaired, or void, by reason of such property not being assessed, or advertised, in the name or names of the lawful owner or owners thereof, provided the same shall be advertised as above directed, or by reason of the amount of taxes due thereon not being correctly stated.

Sec. 3. *And be it further enacted,* That in all cases of sales of real property, for taxes due the said Corporation, where such sale shall not have been made according to law, and void, it shall be lawful for the said Corporation, on the application of the purchaser, or other person entitled under him, to refund and pay to such person or persons, the amount paid by him or them, on account of such purchase; and, also, the subsequent taxes accrued and paid on the said property, and to re-assess the amount of taxes so refunded, on the property on which the same shall have accrued, which shall be collected in the manner as provided by law for the collection of other taxes, at any time after the first day of January next, after the same shall be so re-assessed.

SEC. 4. *And be it further enacted*, That it shall be lawful for the said Corporation, where there shall be a number of lots assessed to the same person or persons, to sell one, or more, of such lots, for the taxes and expenses due on the whole; and, also, to provide for the sale of any part of a lot, for the taxes and expenses due on the said lot, or other lots assessed to the same person, as may appear expedient, according to such rules and regulations as the said Corporation may prescribe.

SEC. 5. *And be it further enacted*, That in case of the death, resignation, or inability to serve, of any commissioner of election, it shall be lawful for the Mayor, or in case of his absence, or inability to perform that duty, for the Register of the city, to make an appointment in writing, to fill any such vacancy, which appointment shall be returned to the Register, with the return of such election.

SEC. 6. *And be it further enacted*, That the proprietor or proprietors of lots which may be sold under the provisions of this act, shall be allowed the right of redemption, in the same manner, and

according to the like restrictions, contained in the
act to which this is a supplement.

Sec. 7. *And be it further enacted,* That public notice of the time and place of sale, of any real
property chargeable with taxes, in Georgetown or
Alexandria, in all cases hereafter, shall be given
once in each week, for twelve successive weeks,
in some one newspaper printed in each of said
places, and in the National Intelligencer, in which
shall be stated the number of the lot or lots, or
parts thereof, intended to be sold, and the value
of the assessment, and the amount of the taxes due
and owing thereon.

Sec. 8. *And be it further enacted,* That if, before the day of sale, advertised as aforesaid, the
owner, his agent or attorney, shall not pay the
amount of taxes, with all costs thereon assessed,
said lots, or so many as may be sufficient to dis-
charge the same, shall be sold, for cash, and to the
highest bidder paying therefor; a certificate from
the proper officer shall be issued, setting forth that
he is the purchaser, and the amount paid by him;
and if, at the expiration of twelve months from
the day of sale, the owner shall not appear, and
pay to the officer who sold the same, the Mayor,
or the purchaser, the amount of the purchase money, and costs, and taxes accruing subsequent to
the sale, and ten per centum interest per annum on
the purchase money, it shall and may be lawful
for a title, in fee simple, at the expiration of said
time, to be made to the purchaser: *Provided,* That
no sale of real estate shall be made but where the
owner or tenant of the property has not sufficient
personal estate out of which to enforce a collection
of the debt due, and where he has personal pro-

perty, it shall be lawful to collect said taxes by distress and sale thereof.

SEC. 9. *And be it further enacted*, That on or before the first day of April next, and every five years thereafter, each of the Corporations of Washington, Georgetown, and Alexandria, shall cause three respectable freeholders, resident in said city and towns, respectively, being previously sworn, to assess and value, and make return of all and every species of property by law taxable, in said Corporations; and, in making their said valuations, they shall determine it agreeably to what they believe it to be worth, in cash, at the time of the valuation.

SEC. 10. *And be it enacted*, That, where any taxes have fallen due, and yet remain unpaid, or where any real estate has been sold by the Corporation of Georgetown or Alexandria, which sale, from any defect of proceeding in relation thereto, has been declared, or is considered void, said Corporation may proceed, and are hereby authorized to collect said taxes by sale of the real estate, liable, agreeably to the provisions of this act, in relation to other cases of collecting taxes hereafter to fall due: *Provided*, That where any person, without notice of the outstanding taxes, has made a bona fide purchase from the legal owner of any real estate, previous to the fifteenth day of May, one thousand eight hundred and twenty-four, said real estate, so acquired, shall not be liable for the taxes due and owing previous to said purchase.

SEC. 11. *And be it further enacted*, That all titles to property conveyed, as aforesaid, on sales for taxes, made in either of said places, shall be by deed from the Mayor, under the seal of the Corporation; which said conveyance shall be effectual in law, to convey the title, the requisition of this act having been complied with.

SEC. 12. *And be it further enacted*, That, on any lot, or lots, or part of a lot, liable for taxes, as aforesaid, being sold, the amount, over and above the tax, cost and charges, due upon the same, shall be paid over, on application, to the owner of said property.

SEC. 13. *And be it further enacted*, That, where the payment of any taxes shall be made or enforced against any tenant, it shall not be lawful for the owner of said property, so made liable for the taxes, to recover of the tenant any rent for the property; but the same shall remain in his possession a lien for the debt, until such time as the rent accruing shall have discharged the same; and the said tenant shall be entitled to charge twenty-five per centum against the landlord, on the amount of the taxes so paid or enforced against him, except where he may have been previously in arrears for his rent.

SEC. 14. *And be it further enacted*, That, in all cases of any nuisance affecting, in the opinion of the board of health, the healthiness of the city of Washington, or inhabitants contiguous thereto, which may exist on any lot belonging to the United States, it shall be lawful to have the same removed, in the same manner, and under the same rules and regulations, that nuisances on private property are removed; and the expense of such removal or correction shall be defrayed out of any moneys in the hands of the city commissioner, for the sale of the public property in said city.

Washington, May 26, 1824.

Approved: JAMES MONROE.

RATE OF TAXES.

The rate of taxes, on real and personal property within the City of Washington, is one-half of one per cent. per annum, on the estimated value thereof. The following are subject to a specific tax:

per ann

Male slaves, between 15 and 45, owned by residents	$2
Female slaves, do. do.	1
Male slaves, between 15 and 18, owned by non-residents,	12
Male slaves, over 18, owned by non-resid'ts	20
Female slaves, over 15, do.	2
Coach,	15
Chariot, post chariot, and post chaise,	12
Phaeton, and coachee with pannel work in upper part,	9
Coachee, with framed posts and top,	6
Curricle, chaise, chair, sulkey, or any two wheeled carriage on iron or steel springs,	3
Four wheeled carriages with frame posts, and top, and on wooden spars,	2
Hacks of resident owners,	10
Hacks owned within the District, but without the city limits,	20
Hacks owned without the District,	50
Wagons owned by residents,	5
Carts and drays, do.	2
Wagons owned by non-residents,	15
Carts and drays do.	6
Male dogs,	1
Female dogs,	5
Licenses to Tavernkeepers,	60
do. Retailers, (of less than a pint,)	50

Licenses to Retailers, (of not less than a pint,) $10
  do. for selling porter, ale, beer, & cider,   15
  do. to Auctioneers,   -   -   - 100
  do.   Billiard tables, -   -   - 100
  do.   Theatrical and other amusements,
          per day,   -   -   -   5
  do.   Confectioners, who sell cordials &
          wines,   -   -   -   10
  do.   Brick-kilns,   -   -   -   1
  do.   Slaughter-houses,   -   -   1
  do.   Hawkers and pedlars,   -   -   35
  do.   Dry goods,   -   -   -   10

LIST OF PUBLIC PLACES, &c.

Showing where they are situated.

General Post Office, btw E and Fn and 7 and Sw
City Post Office, east end of general post office
Patent Office, 2d floor gen post office
Clerk of Supreme Court's office, n wing capitol,
  1st floor
Clerk of Circuit Court's office, east wing city hall
Marshal's office,   ditto
Judge of Orphans' Court, west wing city hall
Register of Wills,   ditto
Mayor's office,   ditto
Register's office,   ditto
Council Chambers,   ditto
Sealer of Weights and Measures, s side Pen av
  btw 12 and 13w
Branch of the U S .Bank, n e corner Pen av & 14w
Patriotic Bank, s w corner Dn and 7w
Bank of Washington, e side New Jersey av btw
  B and Cs Capitol Hill
10

Pages 104 -105 missing in the original copy

Bank of the Metropolis, corner Fn and 15w opposite the treasury department

Franklin Insurance Company, Lenox's Row, Pen av btw 9 and 10w

Washington Asylum, square 448, 7w btw M & Nn

Orphan Asylum, w side 7w btw H and I n

Tobacco Inspection warehouse, 3e btw M and Ns near the Eastern Branch

Washington Assembly Rooms, (Carusi's,) corner Cn and 11w near the Tiber

Washington Library, old Masonic hall, w side 11w btw C and Dn

Western Burying Ground, square 109, btw S and Tn and 19 and 20w

Eastern Burying Ground, square 1026, btw H and I n and 13 and 14e

Episcopalian Burying Ground, near the Eastern Branch upper bridge

Episcopalian (new) Burying Ground, square 276, btw 12 and 13w and R and Sn

Catholic Burying Ground, near the north end of 3w outside the city limits

County Jail, En back of and near the city hall

St. John's Church, (Mr. Hawley's) corner Hn and 16w opposite President's square

Christ Church, (Mr. Allen's) Gs btw 6 and 7e N Yard

First Presbyterian Church, (Mr. Post's) 4½w near the city hall

Second Presbyterian Church, (Mr. Baker's) New York avenue btw 13 and 14w

Dr. Laurie's Church, (Presbyterian) s side Fn btw 14 and 15w

First Baptist Church, (Mr. Brown's) corner I n and 19 west

Baptist Church at Navy Yard, (Mr. Neal's)

Methodist Church at Navy Yard, (Mr. Ryland's.)
Unitarian Church, n e corner Dn and 6w
St. Patrick's Church, (Mr. Matthews') n side Fn
    btw 9 and 10w
St. Peter's Church, (Mr. Lucas') 2e btw C and Ds
St. Vincent's Asylum, orphan and day school, cor-
    ner Gn and 10w
Friends' Meetinghouse, n side I n btw 18 and 19w
African Church at Navy Yard, (Mr. Smith's) 4e
    btw Vir av and Gs
Navy Magazine, on marine hospital reservation,
    Eastern Branch
Navy Hospital, corner 10e and Pen av
Marine Barracks, square 927, btw G and I s and
    8 and 9e
Union Street, runs from M to Os btw 4 1-2 and 6w
    Greenleaf's Point
Davidson's wharf, western termination of Gn
Hamburgh wharf, near the glass house, s end 20w
Lenox's wharf, end of 13 1-2w near Washington
    bridge
Van Ness's wharf, termination of 17w
Cana's wharf, termination of 7w
Coombe's wharf, near the navy yard, E. Branch
Smallwood's wharf,   ditto
Brewery, s end of N Jer av Eastern branch
Glass House, near the southern termination of 20w
Columbian College, near the north end of 14w
Washington City College, corner An Capitol Hill
Medical College, corner En and 10w
Eastern Public School, corner Ds and 3e
Western   do.   corner Gn and 14w
Masonic Hall, corner 4 1-2w and Lou av opposite
    city hall
Masonic Hall, Vir av btw 4 and 5e N Yard
Botanic Garden, opposite west front of the capitol

ADVERTISEMENTS.

www.ingramcontent.com/pod-product-compliance
Lightning Source LLC
Chambersburg PA
CBHW060806110426
42739CB00032BA/3117